Take a Spare Truss

Tips for Nineteenth Century Travellers

Compiled by SIMON BRETT

SPHERE BOOKS LIMITED
London and Sydney

First published in Great Britain by
Elm Tree Books Ltd/Hamish Hamilton Ltd 1983
Collection copyright © 1983 by Simon Brett
Published by Sphere Books Ltd 1984
30–32 Gray's Inn Road, London WC1X 8JL

Book design by Norman Reynolds

TRADE
MARK

Printed and bound in Great Britain by
Cox & Wyman Ltd, Reading

Contents

To Michael Motley,
who gave me the idea

Introduction

THERE were no aeroplanes to fly them off on fortnight package
tours. There was no air-conditioning. The water was dubious, the
food was foreign and the natives were quite possibly hostile. And
yet throughout the nineteenth century the British and American
travelled all over the world.

First went the pioneers and explorers; then, in their wake, the tourists,
clutching their pocket guide-books, their red-bound Murrays and
Baedeckers, eager for new sights and experiences. The world was opening
up and they didn't want to miss a bit of it.

Travellers' tales came back to the home country and from the
experiences of the pioneers travellers' tips were handed on. It is these tips
that provide the subject-matter of this book. In selecting them I have
extended the strict definition of the nineteenth century up to the First
World War, after which accelerating 'progress' and new attitudes changed
everything irrevocably.

Some of the difficulties faced by nineteenth century travellers still
trouble us today. Package tourists still have problems with foreign food,
'foreign tummy', unaccustomed heat, the menace of mosquitoes and the
intractable 'foreignness' of foreigners.

The urgency of other difficulties has passed. Today people worry less
about keeping their cholera belts in place, having their copies of Byron's
Don Juan impounded by the Customs, waterproofing their shoes or
choosing the right colour beads to give to the natives.

Many of the tips on such subjects are included for their anachronistic
quaintness, but there is no intention to ridicule their writers. The pioneers

were all men of remarkable bravery and there is an astonishing wealth of experience and common sense in works like Sir Francis Galton's *The Art of Travel* or the deliciously named *Shifts and Expedients of Camp Life*. The writing frequently shows great wit, and the characters of men like Mansfield Parkyns and Dr William Kitchiner shine vividly across more than a century and a half. This book's title, taken from Kitchiner's *The Traveller's Oracle; or, Maxims for Locomotion* is typical of his bluff, no-nonsense approach to any subject.

But what comes across most forcibly to me from all the items in the book is the confidence of the society they reflect. It's there in the American writers, but even more in the British. When they wrote, the British Empire was a reality, the maps were lavishly splashed with red, and they took it for granted that they came from the greatest nation on earth. Their confidence transcended mere racism. All of them shared the sense of superiority expressed by Mrs C. E. Humphries over 'those countries which we honour with our distinguished presence in our little trips.'

In the preparation of this book I would like to thank the staff of the British Library and the London Library (whose Topography section proved to be an Aladdin's Cave of suitable gems). I am also indebted to Virginia Bell for her help on the research, and to Celia and Jan for their help with the typing.

Author's Note

A number of frequently quoted sources in this collection are credited in abbreviated form. The full titles are as follows:

Aspinall: *West Indies* — *Aspinall's Pocket Guide to the West Indies*, 1907

Baker: *Abyssinia* — Sir Samuel Baker: *The Nile Tributaries of Abyssinia*, 1867

Bremner: *Russia* — Robert Bremner: *Excursions in the Interior of Russia*, 1840

Chambers — T. K. Chambers: *A Manual of Diet in Health and Disease*, 1876

Cobbett — William Cobbett: *The Emigrant's Guide*, 1829

Cumming: *South Africa* — Roualeyn Gordon Cumming: *Five Years of a Hunter's Life in the Far Interior of South Africa*, 1850

Galton — Sir Francis Galton: *The Art of Travel*, 1867

Harford — Charles Forbes Harford, M.A., M.D.: *Hints on Outfit for Travellers in Tropical Countries*, 1911

Hull: *India* — Edmund C. P. Hull: *The European in India*, 1878

Johnston — H. H. Johnston: *Hints on Outfit*, 1889

Kitchiner — William Kitchiner, M.D.: *The Traveller's Oracle; or, Maxims for Locomotion*, 1827

Levinge — Godfrey Levinge: *The Traveller in the East*, 1839

Lord & Baines	W. B. Lord & T. Baines: *Shifts and Expedients of Camp Life*, 1876
Marcy	Captain R. B. Marcy: *The Prairie and Overland Traveller*, 1860
Parkyns: *Abyssinia*	Mansfield Parkyns: *Life in Abyssinia*, 1853
Satow & Hawes: *Japan*	E. M. Satow & Lt. A. G. S. Hawes: *A Handbook for Travellers in Central and Northern Japan*, 1881
Tangye	Richard Tangye: *Reminiscences of Travel*, 1883
Terry: *Japan*	T. Philp Terry: *Terry's Japanese Empire*, 1914

In addition, the Murray and Baedecker *Handbooks for Travellers* are referred to simply as 'Murray' and 'Baedecker'.

General Rules

COMPLETE EQUIPMENTS FOR EXPLORERS AND TRAVELLERS

Manufactured by

S. W. SILVER & CO.

CORNHILL, LONDON.

S. W. SILVER & CO.'S
"PANDORA"
SLEEPING BAG,
Covered Waterproof Material.

As Manufactured by them for the various Arctic Expeditions.

Portable Furniture for Camp Life.   Patent Water Bottles.
Patent Filters.   Patent Guns, Rifles, and Revolvers.

Complete Illustrated Catalogues on application to

S. W. SILVER & CO. and BENJ. EDGINGTON, LTD.,

Sun Court, 67, Cornhill, London, E.C.

The ideal traveller is a temperate man, with a sound constitution, a digestion like an ostrich, a good temper, and no race prejudices.

William Henry Crosse, M.D.:
Medical Hints, 1906

Solitary Travellers.—Neither sleepy nor deaf men are fit to travel quite alone. It is remarkable how often the qualities of wakefulness and watchfulness stand every party in good stead.

Francis Galton:
'The Art of Travel', 1867

Hint before starting

The traveller should never omit visiting any object of interest whenever it happens to be within his reach at the time, as he can never be certain what impediments may occur to prevent him from carrying his intentions into effect at a subsequent period.

Murray's Handbook for Travellers in the Ionian Islands, Greece,
Turkey, Asia Minor and Constantinople, 1840.

However, as the *Sudden Death* of a Traveller, if intestate, would occasion irremediable distress and disputes in his Family; — if he consult only his own Tranquillity, (and the preservation of *Peace of Mind,* is more preventive of the Disorders and even the decays of our Body, than the most careful precautions against unfavourable Seasons, or unwholesome Diet!) he will certainly make his *Will* before he leaves Home.

William Kitchiner, M.D.:
The Traveller's Oracle; or, Maxims for Locomotion, 1827

What to Take

Closely-fitted, well-made cases afford great trouble to thieves, and gaping packages, with partly-exposed contents, invite robbery. Boxes which are *screwed* down are more secure than nailed boxes, as thieves are frequently not provided with screw-drivers.

Charles Forbes Harford, M.A., M.D.:
'Hints on Outfit for Travellers in Tropical Countries', 1911.

Food Box. It need hardly be said that the box and every receptacle in it should be kept scrupulously clean. Slovenliness in this respect is unpardonable. There are quite sufficient risks to life in Central Africa without running the risk of poisoning by putrefying food.

Harford

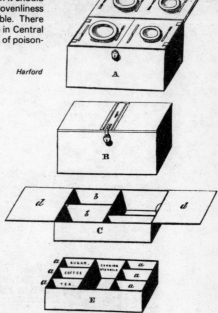

A tent is the first requisite, the old cities and places of the greatest interest being frequently distant from the modern town or khans; and a good tent makes the traveller quite independent of the state of health of the town. It is desirable that the tent should be of waterproof material.

Sir Charles Fellowes:
'Journal Written During an Excursion in Asia Minor', 1839.

A bed pan would also be useful, though this would be rather too large for the special medical case, and something of the kind might be improvised in case of emergency.

Harford

14

Articles of consumption, calculated for a six months' journey for each white man —

Tea and coffee, 9 lbs; tobacco, 6 lbs; salt, 6 lbs; pepper, 1 lb.............22 lbs
Brandy or rum, occasionally served out.................................6 lbs
White sugar, 2 lbs; arrowroot, 1 lb; dried onions, etc., 3 lbs...............6 lbs
Ammunition for small-bored rifles, with reserve powder and caps.........9 lbs
Bags, 6 lbs..6 lbs

49 lbs

Articles of consumption, calculated for six months, for each black man —

Tobacco, 6 lbs; salt, pepper, etc., 5 lbs.................................11 lbs
Presents which will have to be made him from time to time..............6 lbs

17 lbs

Galton

I once travelled with a party of New Yorkers *en route* for California. They were perfectly ignorant of everything relating to this kind of campaigning, and had overloaded their waggons with almost everything except the very articles most important and necessary; the consequence was, that they exhausted their teams, and were obliged to throw away the greater part of their loading. They soon learned that Champagne, East India sweetmeats, olives, etc., etc., were not the most useful articles for a prairie tour.

Captain R. B. Marcy:
'The Prairie and Overland Traveller', 1860

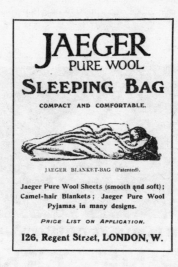
Do not be induced to encumber yourself with one of those ornamented, highly-polished, useless abominations popularly known as hunting knives; they are worse than useless, and serve only to exasperate the owner.

W. B. Lord & T. Baines:
'Shifts and Expedients of Camp Life', 1876

Two most necessary items of any African outfit, however small, are a portable table and a stout portable chair, and it would be better if the traveller took two or three chairs with him (as they are very light and portable) so as to be able to offer a seat to any native of importance who may visit his tent — an attention generally much appreciated.

H. H. Johnston:
'Hints on Outfit', 1889

A quart syringe for injecting brine into fresh meat is very necessary. In hot climates, the centre of the joint will decompose before the salt can penetrate to the interior, but an injecting syringe will thoroughly preserve the meat in a few minutes.

Sir Samuel Baker:
'The Nile Tributaries of Abyssinia', 1867

When about to start on a sledge journey, a certain number of useful matters will be required in addition to those already mentioned.

A few green or blue gauze or tarlatan veils, to protect the eyes from the glare of the snow, will be found of the greatest value. In the absence of these, sledge men not uncommonly collect a quantity of the deposit of black found in the sconces of the lamps. This they mix with grease, and with it black the eyelids and upper part of the face. This expedient, although not equal to a veil, is far better than nothing. We have made use of green glass spectacles, but found them next to useless, as the glasses soon became coated with ice, formed from the condensed vapour given off with the breath. Never travel without a small pocket mirror; by its aid you can discover at once whether your nose or ears are becoming frost bitten, and can act accordingly.

Lord & Baines

17

To accelerate loading, the hunter ought to have his balls stitched up in their patches, and well greased before taking the field. This was my invariable custom: I found it a great convenience, and after a little practice I could load and fire in the saddle, although riding in rough ground at a swingeing gallop.

Cumming: South Africa

As regards food for the mind I cannot too strongly recommend all travellers to supply themselves with quantities of light litera-ture. By "light", I do not mean frivolous in character, but devoid of great material weight, so that it can be easily packed and readily transported. There are a great many standard works now published in cheap editions in paper covers, and these, together with a supply of good novels, sensational tales, old magazines, and reviews, should be taken. Although the traveller should endea-vour to supply himself with books that are worth reading and re-reading, still, it is astonishing with what pleasure he will peruse the veriest rubbish in the wilderness, and really crave for anything that may serve to distract his mind at times from the savagery around him.

Johnston

Many a man has been killed unnecessarily by not having with him a pistol or revolver. If one is pulled down by a beast, unless killed outright there is always a chance to slip a pistol from your belt and get in two or three quick shots. This requires little movement. To draw a knife and plunge it into an animal draws his attention and incites immediate attack.

The Harvard Travellers Club 'Handbook of Travel', 1917

We cannot leave this topic altogether, however, without adding a note of advice for our travelling countrymen, regarding the necessity of providing themselves with good introductions, before coming here. Englishmen are always too negligent of this. We have known some set out on the tour of Europe without a single letter, beyond a pretty substantial one from Coutts's or Herries's! Now, without recommending the German system, which is to get a trunk-full of letters, when they can be got, and to deliver every one of them, even should there be one hundred and twenty (the number brought over by a recent visitor when he came to make a book about us), we should advise the stranger who wishes to enjoy his visit to St. Petersburg, to furnish himself with at least the twentieth part of the German allowance; and if but one half of these are as well attended to as ours were, he will long look back with pleasure to the happy and instructive hours enjoyed on these distant shores.

Without introductions, no stranger can make his way in the Russian capital; with them, he will be loaded with attentions. Many Englishmen who come here are so coldly welcomed that they go away disappointed with the people and the country. But they are themselves to blame for having

found St. Petersburg naught and unprofitable. A single good letter would have enabled them to spend their time both instructively and agreeably. Travellers passing by Berlin cannot do better than provide a few letters there; such, from the present intimacy between the two courts, being the most influential that can be procured.

Were we to follow out the German example we ought, at least, to give a list of all who entertained us, even though the reason given at the commencement of the chapter may prevent us from enlarging on their kindness; but English taste repudiates the trick of giving weight to a work by filling it with eminent names, and thereby throwing the responsibility of its statements on individuals who cannot answer for themselves.

Another fashion — we will not call it a German one, because only *one* German has been found capable of adopting it — is, to use the opportunities which introductions give, for laying bare the sacred privacies of domestic life — for sporting with the afflictions(!) of the family who unsuspectingly gave the ribald jester shelter at their board — and sometimes even for traducing the character of his entertainers! This fashion, however much its adoption might

add to the piquancy of his work, no English writer will ever adopt.

The consideration, however, which principally induces us to refrain from mentioning names in these pages is the danger in which the most respectable individuals have sometimes been involved, by the rashness of travellers in this respect. Foreigners who allude to politics in their works ought never to give the name of any private friend; for many have been exposed to merciless persecution — to the dungeon, and to exile — in consequence of having been mentioned by travellers whose political remarks are unpalatable to the government. To be named in such a work, were it only in the way of well-meant compliment, or thoughtless gratitude, at once exposes the individual to the suspicion of having furnished the obnoxious intelligence, although he may not have opened his lips on politics. There are other continental states also, where the same caution would be necessary: there is an English book of Travels in Southern Italy, which had the effect of compromising some of the first noblemen of the country so seriously, that they were thrown into prison, and never again allowed to breathe the air of freedom.

Robert Bremner:
'Excursions in the Interior of Russia', 1840

Letter of Introduction.

The bearer of this letter is Mr. N. my intimate friend. He visits your town on some important business, and I have no doubt of his success, if you will have the kindness to assist him with your advice and support. When you know him, his merit will recommend him to you sufficiently: and, therefore, as I know his good qualities and the friendship you have for me, I take the liberty of recommending him warmly to your kindness, especially as my recommendations to you have never been in vain. I am, &c.

Baedecker's Traveller's Manual of Conversation in Four Languages, 1886

What to Wear

Clothes should be adapted in color to suit the environment. Leggin trousers are very useful but in a snake country stout leather leggins must be worn.

In a noisy country shoes should have rope or rubber bottoms. Rope wears better. In an African trip six pair are necessary, besides two pair of stout leather boots, the latter to be used on the march and in snaky districts.

A helmet should be worn in hot countries; elsewhere natives give one the idea.

The Harvard Travellers Club 'Handbook of Travel', 1917

21

One's European dress-coat and frock-coat can often be made to do for a
stay in the Tropics, by having the lining taken out.

Dr. J. F. van Bemmelen & G. B. Hooyer, translated by the Rev. B. J. Berrington:
'Guide to the Dutch East Indies', 1897.

We submit the following advice respecting Continuations:— *the Garter* should be
below the Knee; and Breeches are much better than Trowsers:— the general
adoption of these, which till our late long wars were exclusively used by "The
Lords of the Ocean," has often excited my astonishment:— however convenient
Trowsers may be to the Sailor, who has to cling to slippery shrouds, for the
Landsman, nothing can be more inconvenient; they are heating in Summer, and
in Winter are collectors of Mud: moreover, they occasion a necessity for wearing
Garters. *Breeches* are in all respects much more convenient; these should have the
Knee-band three quarters of an Inch wide, lined on the upper side with a piece of
plush, and fastened with a Buckle, which is much easier than even Double
Strings; and by observing the Strap, you always know the exact degree of
tightness that is required to keep up the Stocking; any pressure beyond that is
prejudicial, especially to those who walk long distances.

Kitchiner

The English combination is unquestionably the best costume, and cannot
be too well recommended as highly practical and convenient in a country,
where one has so frequently to change one's clothing.

Dr. J. F. van Bemmelen & G. B. Hooyer, translated by the Rev. B. J. Berrington:
'Guide to the Dutch East Indies', 1897.

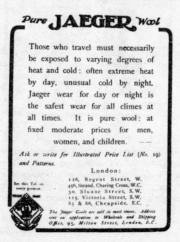

The purpose of a cholera belt is to protect the vital organs of the abdomen from a tendency to chill, which may easily occur in the Tropics in sudden changes of temperature.

Harford

Flannel Belt — It is of much importance in view of the prevalence of diarrhoea and dysentery, that the abdominal organs should be specially protected by a flannel belt, surrounding the body, *and worn day and night.*

The Travellers' Medical and Surgical Guide, 1888.

The cummerbund is a useful article of clothing, especially for men in the evening. It does away with the need for a waistcoat, which often proves hot and uncomfortable, and yet provides the necessary safeguard against chill to the abdominal organs.

William Henry Crosse, M.D., c. 1890.

The well-fitting ventilated pith-helmet, which forms such an effective guard against the mid-day sun, does not equally protect the sides of the head and the back of the neck from its horizontal rays at morn or eve; at such times, therefore, a light curtain of sufficient length should be attached to the rim of the helmet. This curtain at other times can be folded up and fastened round the helmet.

G. E. Dobson, M.A., M.B., F.R.S., c. 1880.

The problem of the influence of the sun's rays upon the body is one which also needs attention, and it has been suggested that the use of materials of red or orange colour may be of benefit in the tropics in the protection of the body from the actinic rays of the sun which are believed to act prejudicially upon the system . . .

A red form of cellular clothing has recently been devised for tropical use, known as non-active cellular. This is worthy of trial.

Harford

Tourists will be well advised not to make themselves too conspicuous with puggarees and similar eccentricities, as cabmen and boatmen naturally consider those who do so to be fair game, and deal with them accordingly. Sun hats are best purchased locally. Blue spectacles are a comfort in Barbados, where the glare from the coral roads is very trying. A waterproof cape will be found convenient, but in ordering it care should be taken to mention that it is for use in the tropics, as beetles have a predilection for inferior caoutchouc.

Aspinall's Pocket Guide to the West Indies, 1907

Braces. — Do not forget to take them, unless you have had abundant experience of belts; for belts do not suit every shape, neither are English trousers cut with the intention of being worn with them. But trousers made abroad are shaped at the waist, especially for the purpose of being worn without braces, if desired. If you use braces, take two pairs, for when they are drenched with perspiration, they dry slowly.

Galton

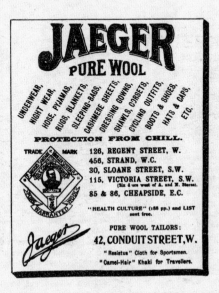

If the traveller inquires whether the Oriental dress be necessary, I answer, it is by no means so; and a person wearing it, who is ignorant of the language, becomes ridiculous. One remark, however, I must be allowed to make on dress in that country — that a person is never respected who is badly dressed, of whatever kind the costume may be, and nowhere is exterior appearance so much thought of as in the East.

Murray:
Egypt. 1847

Ladies should take their usual thin summer dresses, but shun openwork blouses, which are a source of great attraction to mosquitoes, and, owing to the action of the sun, give the wearer the appearance of being tattooed when she appears in evening dress . . . Silk stockings are preferable to cotton, and two pairs of the former worn at the same time render the wearer mosquito proof as far as the region covered is concerned. Sequin dresses should not be taken, as the sequins yield to the great heat and become sticky.

Aspinall:
West Indies

The shoeing of the feet is matter for serious thought. The decks are often temporarily damp — rain, dew, heavy sea, or the washing of the decks are all matters of daily occurrence. On such occasions india-rubber soles, well corrugated, keep the wet out and the wearer on his legs. For those who entertain no pious dread of the heating of their soles there is comfort in the homely golosh. Blacked boots are at a discount on board ship; the pervading dampness makes them leave their blacking in many undesirable ways and places.

W. S. Loftie:
'Orient Line Guide', 1885

Useful Phrases

The tailor.

Who is knocking?
  See who it is. Open the door.

It is your tailor.
  Let him in.

Good morning to you; you have kept me waiting long enough.
  I beg a thousand pardons; but your clothes were not finished.

Well: I will first try on my nankeen pantaloons, and afterwards my trowsers and coat. But where are my waistcoats?

They are not yet finished.
  You shall have them tomorrow without fail.
  These pantaloons are too tight and too short.
  They are not worn now so wide and so long, as they were a fortnight ago.

Is the fashion changed already?

It changes every week, Sir.

Let me now try on the trowsers and the coat.

Your coat is fashionable, both for the material and the colour, and it is very well made.
  We shall see. Look, it does not fit at the waist; the lining does not lie smooth, the sleeves are too tight and the pocket-hole is not wide enough.

Those are slight defects, which can be easily remedied. But the trowsers fit you very well.
  On the contrary, they fit very badly. They are not high enough round the waist: they are tight between the legs, and too wide at the knees.
  I can remedy that, Sir; I will take them away with me, and bring you back everything to-morrow with your waistcoats.

Very well; but mind you do not fail. At the same time you may bring me your bill.

Baedecker's Traveller's Manual of Conversation in Four Languages, 1886

How to Get There

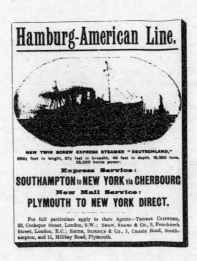

Hamburg-American Line.

NEW TWIN SCREW EXPRESS STEAMER "DEUTSCHLAND,"
686½ feet in length, 67½ feet in breadth, 44 feet in depth, 16,000 tons,
35,000 horse power.

Express Service:
SOUTHAMPTON to NEW YORK via CHERBOURG
New Mail Service:
PLYMOUTH TO NEW YORK DIRECT.

For full particulars apply to their Agents—Thomas Clifford, 22, Cockspur Street, London, S.W.; Shaw, Adams & Co., 9, Fenchurch Street, London, E.C.; Smith, Sundius & Co., 1, Canute Road, Southampton, and 11, Millbay Road, Plymouth.

Ships

A Sailor saying that his Grandfather, his Father, and his Uncle, all died at Sea, a Bystander observed, "Then if I were you, I would certainly never go to Sea." "Why?" said the Seaman; "where did all your Relations die?" "Why, in their beds." "Then," said *Sam Spritsail*, "for the same Reason, if I was You, I would certainly never go to Bed."

Kitchiner

27

Servants —
Female servants shall pay second class fare. Male servants shall pay the
fare of the third class.

Regulations respecting Passengers (on Packets) c. 1830

THE S.S. "ORIENT."

Embarkation.—
If possible, arrange that the painful ordeal of taking leave of your friends and
relations — especially those of your own sex — be got through on shore, and
select a cool-headed male relation or friend to accompany you on board. We have
had oft and bitter experience of parting from those dear to us, and would not
lightly treat so solemn a subject; but the result of our experience is that the agony
of such leave-takings is often needlessly protracted by near relations insisting on
what they call "seeing the last of you." Picture to yourself the confusion on board
one of our large ocean-steamers at the moment some hundred and odd passengers
are embarking! Excited passengers crowding the decks, and elbowing each other
as they distractedly pass and repass on the saloon stairs, with no apparently
definite object, but that of taking violent exercise — perspiring passengers,
hampered with innumerable hand-packages, forcing themselves into wrong cabins
and struggling out again — noise, confusion, scrambling and excitement on
every side — the ship presenting the appearance of a hive when the bees are
swarming! Is this fit time, place, and opportunity for a solemn leave-taking?
Watch the expression of bewilderment on that young fellow's face; he has mislaid
a portmanteau containing his stock of shirts, and, in his search for the same, he
drags about the deck a weeping sister, who hysterically shampoos one of his arms,
as she keeps on begging of him to "write soon," while, with his other arm, he
supports a half-fainting mother, who stops him, at every third step, for "one last
kiss," and the exaction of "a sacred promise" that "happen what may," he will
never, *never* omit to wear flannel next his skin. Would it not have been better, for
all concerned in this little party, if they had wished each other farewell in the
privacy of their own home?

Major S. Leigh Hunt & Alexander S. Kenny:
'Tropical Trials — a Hand-Book for Women in the Tropics', 1883

See the position of your berth, and note whether the vessel is well supplied with sanitary conveniences. The condition of some vessels in this respect is absolutely disgraceful. It is right, however, to say that where this is the case with these conveniences, it is much more frequently the fault of the passengers than that of the officers of the ship, who are, as a rule, only too anxious to secure the utmost order and cleanliness in all departments of the vessel; but this desire is thwarted, and in many cases rendered impossible, in consequence of the filthy habits of some of the passengers.

'General Hints to Emigrants', 1866.

Persons who have never been at sea, fancy that the wooden crib for the bed is too narrow in dimension; but when the ship begins to roll and toss amongst the billows, they soon find the error of the supposition. Were the beds not of circumscribed width, they would be tumbled about from one side to the other, and very likely hove out altogether. Many have their beds widened in harbour, but are glad to reverse matters again on the ocean.

Strangers soon become acquainted with each other; for the natural disposition will show itself there sooner than any where else. How pleasant a voyage is, when a few good-hearted, sensible creatures meet together; and how disagreeable, when they are otherwise, as they most commonly are. He who has had what some will term comforts ashore, finds them not aboard; — then the poor wretch frets himself to death; while the wanderer, who has *roughed out life* in many a dismal climate, laughs at such trifles. Females are always our best companions both on sea and land: although they may be more troubled with sickness in ships than we, still the soft-soothing remark, the resigned state, and sometimes cheerful smile, counterbalance that. The ladies often make cowards of us there; they brave storms with fortitude, at which we tremble.

John Mactaggart:
'Three Years in Canada' 1829

On a Steam-Boat up the Hudson River

We observed nothing to find fault with in this beautiful vessel, but the presence of spit-boxes everywhere — a necessary evil, I suspect, whilst cigars, and tobacco in other shapes, are so generally used as in this country. Smoking of cigars is not, however, allowed in the cabins, or on the decks in the after part of the vessel.

Let us not be too fastidious. Spit-boxes have only disappeared in Scotland within these thirty years, and not even totally, at so late a date.

James Stuart:
'Three Years in America', 1833

The heat of the cabins is not to be described; ours is suffocating: we have two stern windows, but they are of little use, as, the wind being constantly ahead of us, we can get none; and where there ought to be a side-port is a large looking-glass, which only reflects one's dirt and discomfort.

But I could endure all this, were it not for the swarms of cockroaches that infest us; they almost drive me out of my senses. The other day sixty were killed in our cabin, and we might have killed as many more; they are very large, about two inches and a half long, and run about my pillows and sheets in the most disgusting manner. In order to guard myself against them, I am obliged to sleep with a great muslin veil over my face, which adds not a little to the heat and suffocation. Rats are also very numerous. One night Mr. Welby Jackson, one of the passengers, was asleep on the cuddy table, and was woke up by a huge monster running down one of the punka ropes into his shirt, and it was a long time before he could dispossess himself of his unwelcome visitor. The captain keeps a very good table, and has an excellent cook.

Mrs George Darby Griffith:
'A Journey across the Desert', 1845

During the time that you are on board, indulge, if you be a cabin passenger, in as little familiarity as possible with the captain: begin to act upon the American motto (always civil, never servile); you will not find him much disposed to talk, and very rarely will he do anything to give you offence; but, however well you may like him, and however good tempered he may be, it is best to avoid great familiarity; for, recollect you are bound to each other's company for the voyage; you can never be but a few yards asunder; one little crooked word obliterates weeks of kindness; one such word leads to another, and that may become a pain which might have been a very great pleasure.

William Cobbett:
'The Emigrant's Guide', 1829

A ship has been compared to many things — I would give it the title of menagerie; for. besides whales, porpoises, and sharks, you see strange beasts there, which, though inferior in size, do not affect the feelings less. Such is the bed-bug, "the red rover of the sea," and the more agile flea, which always swarm in cotton-laden ships. Both are rare "phlebotomizers." The little dark weevil finding his kingdom in the crevices of the ship-bread "taken from him and given to a stranger," flies for his life, as you raise it to your lips. To these one soon becomes accustomed as well as to the rats, who nightly open avenues through your clothes to the dainty crumb concealed in some of their folds. Sea-sickness may be enjoyed a fortnight together on your back, and also a sudden translation from the berth to the middle of the cabin floor, as the ship may chance to take a sudden lurch — when they are over.

Augustus Kinsley Gardner, M.D.:
'Old Wine in New Bottles', 1849

Knives, Forks and Spoons

I discovered on board ship one remarkable propensity in these articles, namely, a strong pedestrian inclination to walk away to neighbours' berths or dining halls, which inclination could not be curbed by any means but by a strict watch during meals, and a resorting to close confinement as soon as these occasions were past.

General Hints to Emigrants, 1866

Sleeping on Deck

'The only drawback to this was that in the morning we were all literally wet through with the dew, and that the facetious cockroaches amused themselves greatly at our expense; for, awaking in the night, we were sure to find one poking its head into each nostril, others in the ears, mouths, etc., and it was almost impossible to drink, from the myriads which swarmed on the mouths of the leather bottles used for carrying and cooling water. The food we ate, too, and everything else, was full of these disgusting insects; and notwithstanding all the care of the cook, I seldom sat down to dinner without eating two or three by mistake, especially if stewed prunes, to which they nearly assimilate in size and colour, happened to be served.'

Mansfield Parkyns:
Life in Abyssinia, 1853

21. All immoral or indecent acts or conduct, improper liberties or familiarities with the female passengers, blasphemous, obscene, or indecent language, or language tending to a breach of the peace, swearing, gambling, drunkenness, fighting, disorderly, riotous, quarrelsome, or insubordinate conduct and also all deposits of filth or offensive acts of uncleanliness in the between decks, are strictly prohibited.

From the 'Order in Council, for promoting order and health in passenger Ships to any of Her Majesty's possessions abroad': 7th January, 1864.

Useful Phrases

Passage.

Here is my ticket; let me see my cabin immediately.

Send the small things down below.

I hope you do not allow smoking in the saloon?

No, madam; there is a printed notice forbidding it.

Very likely, but somebody is smoking in one of the cabins, all the same; and I beg that you will stop him.

Let me be alone if possible.

Where is the luggage put?

What kind of refreshments do you keep on board?

Are we going to start soon?

We shall have a splendid (rough) passage.

How is the wind? Is it in our favour? Is it against us? Is it getting up? Has it gone down?

How many knots an hour are we going?

Can you get me a folding seat?

What is the extra charge for a deck chair?

The wind is rising.

The sea is very rough.

The motion of the vessel makes me unwell.

I feel very sick (giddy).

Lie down on your back.

Be quite still — don't move.

Close your eyes.

I suffer dreadfully.

Please give me a basin.

Take a little brandy and water.

I feel better.

I think I will go down below.

I would advise you to stay on deck; the stuffy cabin will make you ill again.

Murray's Handbook of Travel-Talk, 1897

Stage Coaches.

Should a person, in Travelling for any considerable distance, and sitting backwards, meet with Companions who close the Windows, and pertinaciously persist in prohibiting any importation of *Oxygen;* — if all arguments on the necessity of Ventilation are unavailing, and your Lungs feel oppressed from the lack of Fresh Air — you may let your Stick or your Umbrella fall (accidentally) against one of the Windows; *i.e.* if you are of opinion that it is more advisable to give a Glazier 3s. to replace a pane of Glass, than it is to pay double that sum for Physic to remove a Pain in your Head, which you will otherwise get by breathing Foul Air.

Kitchiner

. . . Take especial care never to travel post just before or immediately after a great man; should even a corporal with despatches come up while you are changing horses, he will assuredly take yours as a matter of course if there are no others; under such circumstances it will be prudent to submit, and that quietly.

Murray:
Finland and Russia, 1849

Improvements in the mechanism of Modern Carriages, by which they are made to convey a person from place to place almost without giving him a sense of motion, may be one of the circumstances that have contributed to the increased prevalence of Nervous and Bilious Complaints, which originate in a great degree from an indulgence in Lassitude and Languor. The notion of taking *Exercise* upon Springs of such construction, is scarcely less absurd, than that of taking an *Airing* with all the windows closed!

Valetudinarians who wish to derive all the good effects from the Exercise of riding in a Carriage, must not be super-curious about having it suspended on extremely elastic Springs. The Jolting of strong Springs is a salutary concussion, which is extremely convenient to Nervous, Indolent, and Infirm persons who do not take other Exercise, and must be classed among the most agreeable of Anti-bilious remedies.

The Coachmaker's usual phrase of commendation — that such a Carriage "is as easy as a Boat," should be a prohibition to Invalids against purchasing it; who should prefer a Carriage with Strong Springs, that will give them as good a shaking as Equestrian Agitation.

John Jervis, An Old Coachman:
'The Horse and Carriage Keeper's Oracle', 1827

Maxim Forty seventh.
There are two methods of mail-coach travelling, the generous and the sparing. I have tried both, and give my voice decidedly for the former. It is all stuff that you hear about eating and drinking plentifully inducing fever, etc., during a long journey. Eating and drinking copiously produce nothing, mind and body being well regulated, but sleepiness, and I know no place where that inclination can be indulged less reprehensibly than in a mail-coach, for at least sixteen hours out of the twenty-four. In travelling I make it a point to eat whenever I can sit down, and to drink (ale) whenever the coach stops. As for the interim, when I can neither eat nor drink, I smoke if upon deck, and snuff if inside.

N.B. — Of course I mean when there is no opportunity for flirtation.

Mr. O'Doherty:
'Blackwood's Magazine' c. 1820

Useful Phrases

One of the horses has just fallen down.
  Is the driver hurt?
  Yes, he is hurt.
  Let us step out to his assistance, and dress his wound.
  I always carry with me everything that is requisite in such accidents.
  Reach me my small casket. In this casket are bandages of linen, good plasters, Cologne water, fine parchment, brandy, two viols, the one filled with fresh and the other with salt water (I take care to replenish them every morning), a third viol with *eau de Luce*, and a bottle with the juice of unripe grapes, or wine-vinegar.
  The coachman has fainted; apply the smelling bottle with *eau de Luce* to his nose.
  Disengage the coachman from the horse.
  He has broken a leg.
  He has broken an arm.
  Let us take him into the carriage.
  His head is bruised.
  He has a large swelling upon his head. Ought we not to apply a piece of money to it to make it go down?
  By no means! Your proposal is of such a nature, it would be dangerous to comply with it.
  I will only apply some water and salt to the contusion; or Cologne water mixed with fresh water.

Madame de Genlis:
'Manuel de Voyageur; or, The Traveller's Pocket Companion', 1816

Trains

Numberless advices have been issued to the public for the avoidance of railway accidents so far as these depend upon the passenger himself. As regards those accidents which are beyond the control of the passenger, it has been wittily remarked, that "absence of body" is to be preferred to "presence of mind" in a collision. Still, much may be done to lessen the effects of a calamity when it does occur, by the preservation of a cool head; and the following rules of Dr. Lardner, applicable to accidents of both kinds, are worthy of being carefully kept in mind:—
  Rule I. Never attempt to get into or out of a railway carriage while it is moving, no matter how slowly.
  Rule II. Never sit in any unusual place or posture.
  Rule III. It is an excellent general maxim in railway travelling, to remain in your place, without going out at all until you arrive at your destination. When this cannot be done, go out as seldom as possible.
  Rule IV. Never get out at the wrong side of a railway carriage.
  Rule V. Never pass from one side of the railway to the other except when it is indispensably necessary to do so, and then not without the utmost precaution.

Rule VI. Express trains are attended with more danger than ordinary trains. Those who desire the greatest degree of security should use them only when great speed is indispensable.
  Rule VII. Special trains, excursion trains, and all other exceptional trains, are to be avoided, being more unsafe than the ordinary and regular trains.
  Rule VIII. If the train in which you travel meets an accident by which it is stopped at a part of the line or at a time where such a stoppage is not regular, it is more advisable to quit the carriage than to stay in it; but, in quitting it, remember Rules I., IV., and V.
  Rule IX. Beware of yielding to the sudden impulse to spring from the carriage to recover your hat which has blown off, or a parcel dropped.
  Rule X. When you start on your journey, select if you can a carriage at, or as near as possible to, the centre of the train.
  Rule XI. Do not attempt to hand an article into a train in motion.
  Rule XII. If you travel with your private carriage, do not sit in it on the railway. Take your place, by preference, in one of the regular railway carriages.
  Rule XIII. Beware of proceeding on a coach road across a railway at a level-

crossing. Never do so without the express sanction of the gatekeeper.

Rule XIV. When you can choose your time, travel by day rather than by night; and, if not urgently pressed, do not travel in foggy weather.

From 'Travelling Past and Present', ed. Thomas A. Croal, 1877

TERRA FIRMA!

Life on board a "Pullman" train is almost more peculiar than life on board ship. My party were fortunate enough to secure a cabin partitioned off from the rest of the carriage; but the remainder of the sleeping berths have no partitions, being separated merely by curtains. Inexperienced travellers are apt to forget this, and sometimes cause much amusement in consequence. One morning I heard a young lady complaining to her mamma that she could not find her stockings, a remark eliciting numerous offers of assistance from all parts of the carriage. A neighbouring compartment was occupied by a lady and gentleman, the former of whom was deaf, and with the peculiarity often observable in deaf people, she imagined everyone else was deaf as well; the consequence being that there were no secrets in that cabin. Every carriage has a negro attendant, whose duty it is to make the beds and attend to the lavatories, the ladies' and gentlemen's lavatories being at opposite ends of the carriage. At half-past nine o'clock Sambo begins to prepare the beds, and soon after ten almost everyone has retired, and, as fortunately there are no decks to be paced, sleep soon comes to the weary. Arrangements are made for three meals a day, the train stopping at stations convenient for the purpose, and notice being given half-an-hour before. Half-an-hour is allowed for each meal, the invariable charge being one dollar. As the train stops a general stampede is made toward the dining-room, the position of which is unmistakable, for at the door stands a negro, with a face devoid of expression, vigorously sounding a gong. As each person passes in he pays his dollar, and makes a rush to the end of the room, where the cook is usually stationed. And now happy is he who possesses the Yankee's qualification for a good diner-out, for unless he has a long arm, a quick eye, and a silent tongue, he is likely to come off with much less than a dollar's worth. The experienced traveller, before sitting down, gathers all the dishes before him, within arm's length, and then proceeds to attack them *seriatim,* or sometimes all at once. Indeed, I think a man of naturally generous disposition, would be made utterly selfish by twelve months' travelling on American railroads. As soon as the half-hour has gone, the guard calls out with a shrill, nasal, Yankee twang, "All aboard," and we once more continue our journey.

Richard Tangye:
'Reminiscences of Travel', 1883

Many English tourists in France, especially English ladies, find much to complain of in their railway journeys; indeed, it would often seem as if the railway companies did everything in their power to prevent people from using their lines. Smoking is now allowed in *all* the carriages. It is true that, nominally, passengers can prevent anyone from smoking by an appeal to the guard, but he shrinks from interfering if possible; or, if he takes any notice, the complaining passenger's position in the carriage is thenceforward almost untenable. Worse even than the smoking, and the spitting which is its constant concomitant, are the hot water tins, which may be welcome, especially in the north, during the cold days of December and January, but which are equally forced upon the miserable traveller in the most broiling days of April, or under the hottest Provençal sunshine. No remonstrance, no entreaty, not even any plea of illness, is of the slightest avail, until the day is passed upon which an unalterable regulation allows the *chaufferettes* to be left behind. But the miseries of French travel reach a climax during a hot spring day on the Strasbourg line, in carriages heated to roasting-point by flues of hot air, which parch and excoriate their victims at the time, and leave a legacy of fever and bronchitis behind them.

Augustus J. C. Hare:
'North-Eastern France', 1890

I remember on one occasion making a night journey of some 200 miles in a second-class compartment, and the impression left by my sufferings will not be easily effaced. Large numbers of the natives were at the time moving about in all that part of the country, in consequence of some religious festival. The railway company too, ran no third-class carriages at night, so that all were obliged to avail themselves of the accommodation which, in a moment of rash economy, I had chosen.

The second-class carriages are generally large vans to hold fifty passengers, divided in the middle of every second bench by a wooden bar for the back. Not foreseeing a crowd, I had installed myself on the bench farthest from the engine, laying down rug and cushions, and fondly looking forward to a comfortable as well as inexpensive journey; but at every succeeding station fresh native passengers dropped in, with bundles, baskets, boxes, bunches of plantains, etc., and the carriage gradually filled; first one bench and then another, had its full complement of occupants, until at last my domain began to be encroached upon. First one sleek Hindu, then another, then a couple more, closed in upon me, till

39

cushions, rugs, etc., had to be bundled up, and I was finally reduced to being one of a row.

I am imbued with no instinctive repugnance to Hindus or Asiatics in general, nor do I belong to that class of Englishmen, which, according to Baboo Keshub Chunder Sen, "regards the natives as one of the vilest nations on earth," and who not only "hate the natives with their whole heart, but take a pleasure in doing so." At the same time, I must admit, that my cosmopolitan leanings were put to a severe trial upon this occasion.

Many of the natives are addicted to practices which make them anything but agreeable *compagnons de voyage* in close quarters. In the first place, they lubricate the body with oil, sometimes cocoanut, but often castor or margosa oil; the two latter kinds having a most fœtid and, to a European, a most disgusting and nauseating smell. Secondly, being often fat, the natives perspire very freely, which they can hardly be blamed for, but which intensifies the effect of the anointment.

Another of their habits, to which the European never becomes fully reconciled, is that of chewing a mixture of betel-leaf, tobacco, areka-nut, and chunam (lime), which causes a copious red expectoration, which is freely distributed on all sides, and dyes their teeth of every shade from crimson to jet black. This gives the mouth an appearance, from a European point of view, hideous and revolting, but which among themselves is considered positively beautifying.

But worst of all, is their habit of eructating on all occasions, without the least attempt at restraint. Nothing is more surprising to an Englishman, accustomed to look on such an act as a gross breach of good manners; but the natives argue, that after a substantial meal, this is an appropriate method of venting their satisfaction — as it were by way of grace. Of course, natives who have mixed much among Europeans, would not offend in this way before them, but any of even the most refined would freely do so among his fellow-countrymen or in his own family.

Edmund C. P. Hull:
'The European in India' 1878

Camels

Of all species of fatigue, the back-breaking monotonous swing of a heavy camel is the worst; and, should the rider lose patience, and administer a sharp cut with the coorbatch* that induces the creature to break into a trot, the torture of the rack is a pleasant tickling compared to the sensation of having your spine driven by a sledge-hammer from below, half a foot deeper into the skull.

*[Hippopotamus-hide whip]

Abyssinia

THE DESERT JOURNEY.

The accompanying illustration will serve to show how the ropes and tackle are arranged for the purpose of urging a reluctant camel onward.

Baker:
Abyssinia

EMBARKATION TACKLE.

The hind-legs should not be too angular, but rather straight. The hump should not be too much to the front; rather to the rear is better, as then the saddle is more easily adjusted. The hair should not be too short, as then the animal is more easily injured.

From Directions to Purchasers of Dromedaries, by Linant Bey, engineer-in-chief of dykes and bridges
to the Viceroy of Egypt (c. 1850)

A WRECKED SHIP OF THE DESERT.

Mules

Examining a strange or ill-tempered mule's teeth with a view to ascertaining his age is at times rather a risky operation. To do this, put on a blind, get a halter put on the mule's head, stand well in against the near fore-shoulder, pass the right hand gently up the neck patting the animal as it goes until you are enabled to take a steady firm grip of the root of the ear with your right hand; then, with your left, seize quickly, but tightly, on the upper lip and nose. Do this quickly and resolutely, guarding against a blow from the fore-foot, and you will probably get a glance of the front teeth, or incisors, and see if the corner tooth is temporary or permanent.

Another piece of important information will be gained at the same time, and that is whether the dentition of the upper jaw is free from deformity. It sometimes happens that both mules and horses are what is called overhung or parrot-beaked, which simply means that the upper row of front teeth projects so far beyond the lower that the two rows can by no effort of the animal be brought in contact. This defect is often overlooked, but when present is a fruitful source of loss of condition and consequent weakness, as food, easily gathered by animals with naturally-formed rows of teeth, is all but lost to the unfortunate possessor of a parrot-mouth. See, too, that the tongue is perfect.

Lord & Baines

Asses

Messrs. Huc and Gabet, who were distracted by the continual braying of one of their asses throughout the night, appealed to their muleteer: he put a speedy close to the nuisance by what appears to be a customary contrivance in China, viz., by lashing a heavy stone to the beast's tail. It appears that when an ass wants to bray he elevates his tail, and, if his tail be weighted down, he has not the heart to bray. In hostile neighbourhoods, where silence and concealment are sought, it might be well to adopt this rather absurd treatment.

Galton

Where to Stay

FALMOUTH HOTEL (from a sketch by J. Willis).

As a general rule, it is advisable to frequent none but the leading hotels in places off the beaten track of tourists, and to avoid being misled by the appelation of 'Grand-Hotel', which is often applied to the most ordinary inns.

Baedecker:
Southern France, 1907

Gibraltar is so well known that to offer a description would be intrusive. I shall therefore confine myself to stating that there is but one hotel in the town, where, to use the words of a gentleman who recently sojourned therein, "the traveller will find everything low except the charges." The living is said to be bad; wines worse, beds damp and filled with vermin!

Hints to Overland Travellers
(from India — via Egypt) 1838.

In five hours we reached this Centa de Peralbanegas, an execrable place, where our room serves as a passage to an inner one, unluckily occupied by a large party, who will certainly "murder sleep" tonight. They are now at supper, and actually all eating out of the frying-pan!

Robert Southey:
'Letters Written During a Journey in Spain', 1808.

Chairs and tables are generally supplied at the inns frequented by foreigners. They may also often be procured in remote parts of the interior by asking. A well-instructed servant will be able to obtain these additions to comfort without trouble, if they are to be had. Sometimes a small charge is made for their use, as the master of the inn may have to borrow them.

E. M. Satow & Lieut. A. G. S. Hawes:
'A Handbook for Travellers in Central and Northern Japan', 1881.

Travellers who are not fastidious as to their table-companions will often find an excellent cuisine, combined with moderate charges, at the hotels frequented by commercial travellers.

Baedecker:
Southern France, 1907

Hotels —

Verbal reckonings are objectionable. A waiter's mental arithmetic is apt to be faulty, and his mistakes are seldom in favour of the traveller.

The Eastern Alps, 1883.

We found this inn much cleaner and cooler than the last; there was a very civil Italian waiter, who had been there since it was first built, seven years ago. We had plenty of good water for our tea, and the biscuits, which I before described, were steeped in it, in order to render eating them within the range of possibility.

Mrs. George Darby Griffith:
'A Journey Across the Desert', 1845

The accommodation afforded by the *chalets* of the Alpine herdsmen is generally very inferior to that of the club-huts. Whatever poetry there may be theoretically in a bed of hay, the traveller will find that the cold night-air piercing abundant apertures, the jangling of the cow-bells, and the grunting of the pigs are little conducive to refreshing slumber.

Baedecker:
The Eastern Alps, 1883.

In justice to innkeepers it should be added that fleas are not an indication of filth or slovenliness; the incessant rains drive them into the houses, where the style of floor covering offers them pleasing and impregnable positions.

T. Philip Terry:
'Terry's Japanese Empire,' 1914.

Greece:

The keepers of coffee-houses and billiard rooms (which are now very general), will always lodge a traveller, but he must expect no privacy here. He must live all day in public, and be content at night to have his mattress spread, with some twenty others belonging to the family or other guests, either on the floor or on a wooden divan which surrounds the room. When particular honour is to be shewn to a guest, his bed is laid upon the billiard table; he should never decline this distinction, as he will thereby have a better chance of escape from vermin.

Murray:
The Ionian Islands, Greece, Turkey, Asia Minor and Constantinople, 1840.

Travellers, otherwise strong, are apt to get diarrhoea occasionally, partly from the unaccustomed diet, partly from the water, but very frequently also from the pestiferous state of the provisions for daily retirement in Continental inns. It is worth knowing that in many places, especially in France, the landlady has a small private establishment of her own, quite unobjectionable, of which she will lend the key to favoured guests, especially Britons. In country places gentlemen will do well to worship Cloacina *sub Jove.* For otherwise diarrhoea will keep recurring again and again, easier induced by having occurred before; and not unfrequently it will leave traces of imperfect digestion in the bowels for weeks after returning home.

T. K. Chambers:
'A Manual of Diet in Health and Disease', 1876

The bed-chambers do not correspond with the eating-rooms, either in appearance or accommodation, the whole fitting up and furnishing looking meagre. Beds without curtains — not a bit of carpet in the bedrooms — even water not so plentiful as is requisite, most of all in a warm climate — neither hot nor cold baths in this, one of the two greatest hotels in New York — nor proper accommodation of a different, but still more necessary description, for which a plentiful supply of water is indispensable. I am told the British complain every where of the privations to which they are subjected, from the want of such accommodation. The natives not being much accustomed to it, are not aware of its value.

James Stuart:
'Three Years in America', 1833

At an Hotel at Dedham

A female waiter attended at dinner, a very pretty girl, on whom one of our fellow-travellers, an Irish gentleman, bestowed more notice than is relished, or rather allowed, in such circumstances in this country. He first looked hard at her, and then said to his neighbour at table, but so as to be overheard by all, "What a charming creature." The girl blushed, and did not lose a moment in leaving the room. It happened, fortunately, that there were other waiters in the house. The hotel-keeper did not make his appearance, as we expected, to complain of what he no doubt considered rudeness and familiarity on the part of this gentleman; but another of our stage companions, a resident of Boston, explained to our Irish fellow-traveller the very different manners of the two countries, in relation to houses of public entertainment; that the profession of an innkeeper was considered perfectly respectable here; and that the daughters of innkeepers, though as well educated as the daughters of any other persons in the state, did not consider themselves degraded by attending to the household work in the mornings; and that it was not at all impossible that the female who had been remarked upon so unceremoniously was one of the daughters of the landlord, who, as soon as dinner was over, would dress as smartly as any of the young ladies in the town, and be received on a complete footing of equality in the most respectable families. He therefore recommended to our fellow-traveller to beware of repeating conduct of this kind, as it might happen, that he might find a landlord who would resent it, by turning him out of his house without much warning. Instances of this kind had often happened.

James Stuart
'Three Years in America', 1833

'Patras has two Hotels. The Hotel of Great Britain is the best. The other is called the Hotel of the Ionian Isles.'

Godfrey Levinge:
The Traveller in the East', 1839

47

At Fingal [in Tasmania] we stopped at an hotel, kept by an Irishman married to a Jewess. They presided at either end of the table, and kept us short of food; indeed, I never saw a small joint go so far before. Next day we left the hotel, still hungry, although the charges were quite as high as those at the Great Western Hotel, Paddington.

Tangye

Carbolic acid should always be taken on a journey when the tourist expects to meet with inferior accommodation. A piece of paper sprinkled with a small quantity will relieve the occupant of the room from the offensive odours which not infrequently pervade a Japanese inn.

Satow & Hawes:
Japan

Useful Phrases

Paying the Bill.

I set off to-morrow morning.

Let the bill be made out, if you please.
My bill!

I want my bill; have you made it out?

I wish to settle it over-night.

How much have I to pay?

Give me a bill with the individual charges.

Make out one bill for both (all) of us.

Make out the two bills separately.

Put that down to my account, and this to the other gentleman.

What is the total amount?

What! So much. That is impossible.

It is all right, Sir.

Well! Let us see.

Explain it.

I think there is a little mistake.

An error in the adding up.

We did not have —.

That is not fair.

It is a very high charge, but we must submit to it.

There is your money.

Please receipt the bill.

I want change for a twenty-franc piece.

Give me some small change.

Here is something for the attendance — the chambermaid.

Which is the head waiter?

You must divide that among you; I cannot give tips to everybody.

Murray's Handbook of Travel-Talk, 1897

An English tourist will always do well to remember that his approval or his custom is of no consequence whatever to an hotel-keeper in a quiet French town. Any attention he receives is due to the natural kindness and courtesy of his host and hostess: the only travellers of importance to them are 'Les Messieurs de Commerce,' upon whose patronage their house entirely depends. Therefore, however much they smoke horrible tobacco, spit like fountains, shout whenever they speak, and give themselves the airs of princes, it is necessary to recollect that French commercial travellers are of considerable local consequence, whereas a foreigner, however distinguished at home, is of none whatever.

Augustus J. C. Hare:
'North-Eastern France', 1890

J. Harriot, Esq., Projector of "The Thames Police," and Author of "Struggles through Life," states, that in travelling to America with a great number of Persons in the same conveyance, and learning from their conversation, that the Sleeping-house had but few Beds, which would render it necessary that several should sleep in a Bed; to which Mr. Harriot felt great aversion, but said nothing. Finding at the Sleeping-house that their apprehensions were realised, he opened his baggage and took his Horse Pistols and loaded them in the presence of the Passengers, and then placed one of them on each of the Pillows:— When the Passengers asked eagerly what he meant by that? he told them that he had travelled a great deal in many Countries, and had got so much into the habit of it, that he could not Sleep if he did not place a loaded Pistol on each side of his Head. The consequence was, he had all the Bed to himself, as none of them offered to look near it.

Kitchiner

Dealing with Foreigners

A few simple conjuring tricks, and the knowledge of how to show them off, are often of the highest use to travellers in winning the esteem and respect of their temporary hosts.

Johnston

Management of Savages.

General Remarks.— A frank, joking, but determined manner, joined with an air of showing more confidence in the good faith of the natives than you really feel, is the best. It is observed, that a sea-captain generally succeeds in making an excellent impression on savages: they thoroughly appreciate common sense, truth, and uprightness; and are not half such fools as strangers usually account them. If a savage does mischief, look on him as you would on a kicking mule, or a wild animal, whose nature is to be unruly and vicious, and keep your temper quite unruffled.

Galton

On arriving at an encampment, the natives commonly run away in fright. If you are hungry, or in serious need of anything that they have, go boldly into their huts, take just what you want, and leave fully adequate payment. It is absurd to be over-scrupulous in these cases.

Galton

Of all European inventions, nothing so impresses and terrifies savages as fireworks, especially rockets. I cannot account for the remarkable effect they produce, but in every land it appears to be the same. A rocket, judiciously sent up, is very likely to frighten off an intended attack and save bloodshed. If a traveller is supplied with any of these, he should never make playthings of them, but keep them for great emergencies.

Galton

National Flag:—

Without this for the boat on the Nile, a traveller is subject to perpetual annoyance, and to frequent visits from those whose duty it is to prevent smuggling: every European traveller should have the flag of his nation always flying, which will protect him from insult, and save the trouble of going into every town, where he may otherwise be called upon to answer the questions of the authorities.

Levinge

Presents and Articles for Payment.—
It is of the utmost importance to a traveller to be well and judiciously supplied with these: they are his money, and without money a person can no more travel in Savagedom than in Christendom. It is a great mistake to suppose that savages will give their labour or cattle in return for anything that is bright or new: they have their real wants and their fashions as much as we have; and, unless what a traveller brings meets either the one or the other, he can get nothing from them, except through fear or compulsion.

The necessities of a savage are soon satisfied; and, unless he belongs to a nation civilised enough to live in permanent habitations, and secure from plunder, he cannot accumulate, but is only able to keep what he actually is able to carry about his own person. Thus, the chief at Lake Ngami told Mr. Andersson that his beads would be of little use, for the women about the place already "grunted like pigs" under the burdens of those that they wore, and which they had received from previous travellers. These are matters of serious consideration to persons who propose to travel with a large party, and who must have proportionally large wants.

Speaking of presents and articles for payment, as of money, it is essential to have a great quantity and variety of *small change,* wherewith the traveller can pay for small services, for carrying messages, for draughts of milk, pieces of meat, &c. Beads, shells, tobacco, needles, awls, cotton caps, handkerchiefs, clasp-knives, small axes, spear and arrow heads, generally answer this purpose.

There is infinite fastidiousness shown by savages in selecting beads, which, indeed, are their jewellery; so that valuable beads, taken at hap-hazard, are much more likely to prove failures than not. It would always be well to take abundance (40 or 50 lbs. weight goes but a little way) of the following cheap beads, as they are very generally accepted, — dull white, dark blue, and vermilion red, all of a small size.

It is the ignorance of what are the received articles of payment in a distant country, and the using up of those that are taken, which, more than any other cause, limits the journeyings of an explorer: the demands of each fresh chief are an immense drain upon his store.

Galton

Though it is no longer customary to make presents, the traveller will probably wish to leave some token of remembrance with those from whom he has received hospitality. For this purpose a few extra pair of pistols, knives, needles, pocket-telescopes, penknives, scissors, pencils, India rubber, well bound blank books, ink-stands, toys for children and ornaments for ladies should be provided. Prints of the Queen, ministers, &c., are acceptable to the British Consular agents, who are generally natives.

Murray:
The Ionian Islands, Greece, Turkey, Asia Minor, and Constantinople, 1840.

It is a safe rule, when a man finds himself alone in the prairies, and sees a party of Indians approaching, not to allow them to come near him, and if they persist in so doing, to signal them to keep away. If they do not obey, and he be mounted upon a fleet horse, he should make for the nearest timber. If the Indians follow and press him too closely, he should halt, turn round, and point his gun at the foremost, which will often have the effect of turning them back, but he should never draw trigger unless he finds that his life depends upon the shot; for as soon as his shot is delivered, his sole dependence, unless he have time to reload, must be upon the speed of his horse.

Marcy

From 'General Rules for the Treatment of North American Indians'

4. Trust to an Indian's *honour*, and you are tolerably safe — you and your goods; but not to his *honesty*, for he will steal the ears off your head, unless you are very skilful in making a *cache*. If in a neighbourhood where there are Indians, you had far better leave your goods in their charge until you come back; you will generally find them safe; but if they find your *cache* — their honesty being doubted, and having no honourable scruples — they will be sure to clean it out.

5. Never appear to be afraid of them.

7. In making presents, take into consideration their wants; only make presents where you may expect a return; they do that with you; and goodness of heart is only thrown away. Never calculate on this last weakness.

8. In making presents for conciliatory purposes, always make them to the head people; never mind the smaller tribes' men. Be sure, however, that it *is* the chief you are making presents to, and not some forward and impudent fellow, who is usually the first to accost you at the outskirts of a village. The chief generally retires on his dignity, and wants to be sought out. Secure the head man's regard, and you need not mind the favour of the smaller ones; but even if you had abundance of goods to distribute, you would be sure to create red blood and heart burnings by one man's present being better than another, or supposed to be, &c.

10. Never allow the natives to eat with you as your equal. As a rule, play the great man with them.

11. If a savage is travelling with you, give him food whenever he wants it. Food given when he wishes it is of ten times more value than when he gets it when he does not need it, or is not hungry. Consult his wishes in this respect.

12. Never attempt to gain anything by force; always by persuasion, argument, and *presents*.

13. Notwithstanding all you will be told about the value of a medical knowledge in travelling among savages, I have generally found it of very little benefit, and frequently, when put in practice, of real detriment. An Indian will never come to you unless when at death's door and he has lost confidence in his own sorcerers. You may give him some medicine, and perhaps in nine cases out of ten the patient dies, as he would have done anyhow. Their professional jealousy is raised, and you are accused by the "medicine men" of killing the person; and the worst of the matter is, it is often believed by the credulous people. If the man recovers, it is rarely that you get the credit of it. It is the medicine men who have

done it. With surgery it is somewhat different. If the operation is one not involving any very serious consequences if unsuccessful, by all means perform it. They then *see* the working of your superior knowledge before their eyes.

14. Be just and firm, patient and equanimous with them. Display no anger or violent and passionate gestures, and never be very prone to notice insults.

15. Never say you will do a thing and not do it. Never threaten to do anything unless you intend to do it.

16. No people notice the weakness and moral shortcomings of a man quicker than savages; therefore beware, especially *in re foeminâ*.

17. Try by all means to learn the customs and social etiquette of the people; for nothing raises you more in their estimation than this knowledge, or enables you to see when you are slighted.

20. Always, and above everything, remember that the hearts of all mankind are the same, and that all the difference between one and another is merely the overlay caused by etiquette, custom, and education; at heart they are the same.

Dr. Brown, Expanded and Amended by Captain Stuart, Before 1860

The manners of the Greeks would be engaging, were it not that they have an air of obsequiousness and insincerity, particularly striking to the eye of an Englishman.

John Cam Hobhouse, Baron Broughton:
'Travels in Albania and Other Provinces of Turkey', 1813

And here again it may be observed, that the theory of equality may be very daintily discussed by English gentlemen in a London dining-room, when the servant, having placed a fresh bottle of cool wine on the table, respectfully shuts the door, and leaves them to their walnuts and their wisdom; but it will be found less palatable when it presents itself in the shape of a hard, greasy paw, and is claimed in accents that breathe less of freedom than of onions and whiskey. Strong, indeed, must be the love of equality in an English breast if it can survive a tour through the Union.

Frances Trollope:
'Domestic Manners of the Americans', 1832

His Majesty was pleased to compliment me on my extraordinary success and skill in hunting, and observed that the medicine of the white man must indeed be strong.

In the course of the evening he amused me with the quaintness of his questions, asking me if my father and mother were alive, how many brothers and sisters I had, if the flocks and herds of my king were extremely abundant, and if his subjects were more numerous than his own. On informing him that our chief was a woman, he seemed much tickled by the disclosure; and when I said that her subjects were as numerous as the locusts, he looked round on his warriors with an evident grin of disbelief, and then inquired of me if all my countrymen could vanquish the elephants as easily as I did. This was a puzzler: so I replied that I could not say; but I knew that the hearts of all my nation were very strong, like the heart of the lion when his cubs are small. The whole assembly was greatly moved by this bright remark, and a general murmur of surprise and admiration extended through the dusky ranks as each man repeated to his neighbour the surpassing courage of my lion-hearted countrymen.

Cumming:
South Africa

Russian Custom-House

Travellers should be particularly careful not to change foreign coin for Russian paper money before they enter Russia. In order to prevent the introduction of forged notes, not only is the importation of paper money forbidden, but if any is found on the person or baggage, it is liable to confiscation, and the owner to fine and imprisonment. This does not apply to silver money, but the exportation of it is equally illegal. Sealed letters, lottery tickets, playing cards, books subject to the censorship, articles of dress which have not been worn, and poisonous drugs, come within the category of prohibited articles; so that a medicine chest is liable to seizure; but it will, of course, be returned, on assuring the authorities that the rhubarb is not intended for his Imperial Majesty's liege subjects, but for your own sweet self. Books, and even maps, will also be set aside to be examined by the censor; these are sometimes made up into a parcel and sealed with lead, and then delivered to the owner, who engages, by signing a paper, to send them to the censor. The penalty for breaking or losing the lead seal is twenty-eight silver rubles, about 4*l.* 10*s.* If a stranger should have any objectionable work with him, for instance, Byron's Don Juan, it will be retained; but, on application, returned to the owner on his leaving Russia. The search is, generally speaking, strict; each article of dross is taken from the portmanteau or imperial, and contemplated with a degree of earnest attention that awakens the most lively anxiety as to its future destination. To ladies this ordeal is peculiarly trying, and a fair author thus feelingly and indignantly alludes to these annoyances. "A black-looking being, with face like a bull-dog and paws like a bear, fumbled and crumbled a delicate *garde-robe* without mercy — stirring up large and small, tender and tough, things precious and things vile, ruthlessly together, to the unutterable indignation and anguish of the proprietor. To witness the devastation of an English writing-desk was a curious sight to an uninterested spectator. First, the lock excited great anger, and was a convincing proof that little was to be done with Bramah by brute force; and, this passed, there ensued as striking an illustration of the old adage of a bull in a china-shop as could possibly be devised. Every touch was mischief. They soiled the writing-paper and spilt the ink; mixed up wax, wafers, and water-colours. Then, in their search for Russian bank-notes, the introduction of which is strictly interdicted, they shook out the blotting-book, whence a shower of letters of introduction, cards of address, and a variety of miscellaneous documents, floated to distant corners of the salle — ransacked

56

the private drawer, of which they were perfectly *au fait* – displaced all the steel paraphernalia, and then crammed them into their wrong places, cutting their fingers at the same time – the only action which afforded the spectator any unmixed pleasure; and now, smarting with the pain, flung down the lid, and left the grumbling owner to gather his scriptural fragments together as he best could. Beyond the writing-desk they did not choose to proceed. It was past the regulation time, and instead of allowing the weary traveller, as is usual in such cases, to take his carpet-bag of necessaries, the smallest article was denied with a stolid pertinacity, which intimated no great sympathy on their parts for the comforts of clean linen." We think this description is not greatly overcharged, and that even a protectionist would advocate free trade when passing the Russian *douane:* indeed, the custom-house usages of most countries are one of "the miseries of human life."

Murray:
Finland and Russia, 1849

Language

English travellers often impose considerable trouble by ordering things almost unknown in German usage, and are apt to become involved in disputes owing to their ignorance of the language.

Baedecker:
The Eastern Alps, 1883.

Good Interpreters are very important: men who have been used by their chiefs, missionaries, &c., as interpreters, are much to be preferred; for so great is the poverty of thought and language among common people, that you will seldom find a man, taken at hazard, able to render your words with correctness. Recollect to take with you vocabularies of all the tribes whom you are at all likely to visit.

Galton

The great words for a stranger are *pashloushti* and *tchitass* — with these two a man may do wonderful things. There are no bells, be it known, unless in foreign houses. When any thing is wanted, therefore, you plant yourself on the head of the stair, and, in your helplessness, roar out *pashloushti* — "Hey! come here!" After a befitting pause, *pashloushti* appears in the shape of an intelligent lad, to whom, having no words to express your wants, you *make signs* explaining what is required, pointing to your boots, to your writing materials, or whatever else your wants may be connected with. The lad listens in silence, for he is too well-bred to stop you in the middle with a torrent of words, as a French garçon would do, and too honest to say he understands you when he does not. He waits patiently, therefore, till he comprehends your dumb show, and then shuffles off with a knowing shake of the head, and a consenting *dassj, dassj* — "yes, yes" — or a mysterious *chorosho, chorosho,* changed

57

sometimes into *dobrüj, dobrüj,* one or other of which is always on their lips, and means "Good — all right — *c'est bon.*" Seldom indeed is the negative *njet, njet,* "No, no," heard on these occasions; for they are much more quick at understanding than most nations. If wise, however, you will add the second word above named, *tchitass, tchitass,* "Quickly, instantly," else you run a great risk of waiting long enough for his return.

Bremner:
Russia

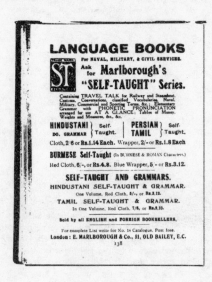

The Servant Problem

TWO BOXES ON ENDS OF POLE.

English servants are in general rather incumbrances than otherwise, as they are usually but little disposed to adapt themselves to new customs, have no facility in acquiring foreign languages and are in general more annoyed by hardships than their masters.

Murray:
The Ionian Islands, Greece, Turkey, Asia Minor, and Constantinople, 1840.

A numerous suite is still requisite; but the wages of servants are so moderate, that a dozen Arabs may be had for what is paid to a valet in England.

Levinge

If without a servant, the first thing after securing rooms is to take one, who may be engaged beforehand by writing to a friend at Malta, or may be found at the door of the lazaretto; where many come to offer their services with letters of recommendation from former masters, which may be read *but not touched*.

Murray:
Egypt, 1847

Most of the Greek servants take care to inform travellers that they were in the service of Lord Byron, and from our experience I should say it would be a rarity to find one who had not been in his Lordship's suite according to his own account.

Octavian Blewitt, c. 1850

Intercourse with Orientals.
The objects and pleasures of travel are so unintelligible to most Orientals that they are apt to regard the European traveller as a lunatic, or at all events a Croesus, and therefore to be exploited on every possible occasion. Hence their constant demands for 'bakshish' (a gift). To check this demoralizing cupidity the traveller should never give bakshish except for services rendered, unless occasionally to aged or crippled beggars.

Baedecker:
The Mediterranean, 1912

While on the subject of pecuniary affairs I must not omit introducing to the traveller a word, with which he will soon be familiar in Turkey — the word is Backsheesh, which means a gratuitous gift of money. There is no service that a Turk can render, no matter how trifling, that he will not expect to receive a backsheesh in return.

Levinge

We would suggest to the traveller to furnish himself with a supply of small silver coins, such as pieces of twenty centimes, easily to be procured at Turin, Genoa, or Milan, which will be useful where such minor services as drawing the curtain from before a picture or opening a door are required.

Murray's:
'Knapsack Guide for Travellers in Italy,' 1864.

The traveller [in Cairo and Alexandria] should keep his eye on the direction taken by the cab, as sometimes the cabman drives straight ahead in complete ignorance of the way and requires to be guided, e.g. by being touched with a stick on the right or left arm according to the turning.

Baedecker:
Egypt, 1902

Upon reaching my camp I found a funny little fellow in the shape of the Bushboy before alluded to awaiting my arrival. My Hottentots had detected his black woolly head protruding from the reeds adjoining the fountain, and had captured him. I presented him with a suit of new clothes and a glass of spirits, and we immediately became and have ever continued the best of friends.

Cumming:
South Africa

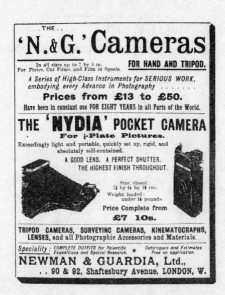
61

A Travelling Servant on Zante

The day following he assisted in getting my luggage on board. When we were nearly ready for sailing, he asked me to advance him a few dollars, and permit him to go on shore for his things. Both these requests I granted him, and I never saw him again.

Levinge

Recollect that the 'dhobi' or Indian washerman has no mercy on your garments. After dipping them in water he twists them up and bangs them on a large stone, collars, ties, and such small articles being done a dozen or more at a time, tied together. There is more madness in his method than method in his madness. So the better the quality of your apparel the longer will be its life at his hands, especially as he is wont to resort to chemicals more than honest soap and elbow-grease to effect his purpose.

Lieut. J. E. Power:
'Vade Mecum for Officers and Civilians Proceeding to India', 1912

A peculiar expression in the eyes of these gentlemen [the Hottentots], and their general demeanour, inclined me to think that their potations had consisted of some more generous beverage than water during the morning's march; and on examining one of my liquor-cases, I found that I was minus a bottle and a half of gin since yesterday. This is a common failing among this monkey-faced race, nineteen in every twenty Hottentots being drunkards, and they have, moreover, not the slightest scruple of conscience as to who is the lawful proprietor of the liquor, so long as they can get access to it. No locks nor bolts avail; and thus on the Bay-road, the high road between Algoa Bay and Grahamstown, a constant system of tapping the admiral is maintained. In this pursuit these worthies, from long practice, have arrived at considerable skill, and it is usually accomplished in the following manner:— If the liquor is in a cask, having removed one of the hoops, a gimlet is inserted, when, a bucket or two of spirit having been drawn off, the aperture is filled with a plug, and, the hoop being replaced, no outward mark is visible. The liquor thus stolen, if missed, and inquiries issued, is very plausibly set down to the score of leakage. A great deal of gin arrives in Grahamstown in square case-bottles, packed in slight red wooden cases. To these the Hottentots devote marked attention, owing to the greater facility of getting at them. Having carefully removed the lid and drained several of the bottles, either by drinking them or pouring their contents into the water-casks belonging to the waggons, they either replace the liquor with water and repack the case again as they found it, or else they break the bottles which they have drained and replace them in the case, at the same time taking out a quantity of the chaff in which they had been packed. This is done to delude the merchant into the idea that the loss of liquor occurred owing to breakage from original bad packing. The risk and damage entailed on the proprietors of waggons and owners of merchandize from the drivers indulging in such a system, on the precarious roads of the colony, may be imagined.

Cumming:
South Africa

Reluctant Servants. — Great allowance should be made for the reluctant co-operation of servants; they have infinitely less interest in the success of the expedition than their leaders, for they derive but little credit from it. They argue thus:— "Why should we do more than we knowingly undertook, and strain our constitutions and peril our lives in enterprises about which we are indifferent?" It will, perhaps, surprise a leader who, having ascertained to what frugal habits a bush servant is inured, learns on trial, how desperately he clings to those few luxuries which he has always had. Thus, speaking generally, a Cape servant is happy on meat, coffee, and biscuit; but, if the coffee or biscuit has to be stopped for a few days, he is ready for mutiny.

Flogging. — Different tribes have very different customs in the matter of corporal punishment: there are some who fancy it a disgrace and a serious insult. A young traveller must therefore be discriminating and cautious in the licence he allows to his stick, or he may fall into sad trouble.

Galton

Natives of the coolie class are often splendid runners, and will often carry a letter or a parcel as far and as fast as an average European on horseback. Did space permit, I could relate many feats illustrating this assertion, but one will suffice.

When engaged in superintending some fieldwork one day, I found myself short of nicotian appliances; and being then an inveterate smoker, at once beckoned to a Tamil coolie, working close at hand, and giving him a written slip, and explaining how things stood, told him to run into Kandy (Ceylon) fourteen miles distant, deliver the note and bring out the required article. It was now near noon, and a present was promised if he was back by seven in the evening. Before the time named, my messenger was back, his face glowing with evident satisfaction at having accomplished the feat.

Hull:
India

A large party of Arabs, none of whom could boast of more than one eye, came forward, and vociferously demanded to be employed. I engaged one of them as a guide, thinking to get rid of their importunities, but I was mistaken, and I then threatened the first who should touch me or my donkey with a sharp blow from the stick I held in my hand; nothing, however, succeeded in quieting them, until I had really carried my last threat into execution. The receiver talked a great deal, and appeared very angry, but, the laugh being against him, he turned and went away. To this decisive commencement on my part I attribute the little incivility I afterwards received while ascending the Pyramids, for, from all accounts, the Arabs about them are a very saucy set.

Mrs George Darby Griffith:
'A Journey across the Desert', 1845

It is always convenient for a stranger at a hotel where the servants are men of colour, to have one of them attached to him, for waiting at table, brushing his clothes, shoes, &c. He will be rendered sufficiently attentive, and even obsequious, by giving him a very trifling douceur on entering the house, and promising him a compliment on going away, provided he does his duty. I attended to this direction on placing myself in Mr. Gadesby's hotel. Jesse was the name of the slave who attended me, and a very good servant he was, and expressed great gratitude for some little attention I had it in my power to show him during a severe but short illness he had. I gave him, on coming away, a douceur quite equal to his services, but I found after leaving Washington, that he had appropriated to himself three pairs of shoes — the whole of my stock.

James Stuart:
'Three Years in America', 1833

Food

SPRATT'S PATENT
SHIP BISCUITS
FOR
HUMAN USE
AND
DOG CAKES
FOR
SLEIGH DOGS
ARE SUPPLIED TO THE
Expeditions of the
Royal Geographical Society.

These SHIP BISCUITS and also
DOG CAKES
WERE SUPPLIED TO
DR. NANSEN
FOR HIS
ARCTIC EXPEDITION.
SPRATT'S PATENT, LIMITED,
24 & 25, FENCHURCH STREET, LONDON, E.C.

On Board Ship

It is best to take your own provisions . . . I would add, some fresh eggs, well packed either in bran or salt; I do not recollect anything else, except a bottle of brandy for the steerage passenger, and a gallon of brandy for the cabin passenger, to be judiciously administered in *bribes* to the *black cook*. He would bid you toss your money into the sea; but he will suck down your brandy; and you will get many a nice thing prepared by him, which you would never get, if it were not for that brandy . . .

Cobbett

Beware of Emigrant Provision Stores

While hinting at the evanescent nature of the tin materials, I cannot urge the same fault against the provisions. The tea had evidently been upon more than one voyage, and if I had had the slightest idea of the dearness of leather in Canada, I should have carried my cheese thither to serve for boot soles, for which purpose it was evidently well adapted.

Chambers' Journal, c. 1860

One day we had very rough weather, with an occasional sea dashing over the deck, along which the dinner was brought from the kitchen. My steward quietly told me to take none of the turtle soup, and I obeyed. After dinner I asked him why he advised me to let the soup pass? He said that as they were coming along the deck a sea came over and washed half the soup out of the tureen, decidedly mixing what was left! Those who partook of the soup remarked that the cook had put rather too much salt to it; but they libelled that useful functionary.

Tangye

Self-Catering

As a rule the inn-keepers object to their kitchen utensils being used for cooking foreign food. A frying pan, and perhaps a gridiron also, will therefore be found extremely useful.

Satow & Hawes:
Japan

I have lived for days upon nothing but raw onions and sun-dried rusks. Nothing is so good a substitute for meat as an onion; but if raw, it should be cut into thin slices, and allowed to soak for half an hour in water, which should be poured off: the onion thus loses its pungency, and becomes mild and agreeable; with the accompaniment of a little oil and vinegar it forms an excellent salad.

Baker:
Abyssinia

FISH — Tinned fish as a rule cannot be eaten without considerable risk in hot climates, and tinned salmon or lobster should especially be avoided. Sardines, however, might be taken with advantage if they are liked.

Harford

The pemmican, which constitutes almost the entire diet of the Fur Company's men in the North-west, is prepared as follows: The buffalo meat is cut into thin flakes, and hung up to dry in the sun or before a slow fire; it is then pounded between two stones and reduced to a powder; this powder is placed in a bag of the animal's hide, with the hair on the outside; melted grease is then poured into it, and the bag sewn up. It can be eaten raw, and many prefer it so. Mixed with a little flour and boiled, it is a very wholesome and exceedingly nutritious food, and will keep fresh for a long time.

The most portable and simple preparation of subsistence that I know of, and which is used extensively by the Mexicans and Indians, is called *"cold flour."* It is made by parching corn, and pounding it in a mortar to the consistency of coarse meal; a little sugar and cinnamon added make it quite palatable. When the traveller becomes hungry or thirsty, a little of the flour is mixed with water and drunk. It is an excellent article for a traveller who desires to go the greatest length of time upon the smallest amount of transportation. It is said that half a bushel is sufficient to subsist a man thirty days.

Jerking Meat.

So pure is the atmosphere in the interior of our continent that fresh meat may be cured, or *jerked,* as it is termed in the language of the prairies, by cutting it into strips about an inch thick, and hanging it in the sun, where in a few days it will dry so well that it may be packed in sacks, and transported over long journeys without putrefying.

When there is not time to jerk the meat by the slow process described, it may be done in a few hours by building an open frame-work of small sticks about two feet above the ground, placing the strips of meat upon the top of it, and keeping up a slow fire beneath, which dries the meat rapidly.

The jerking process may be done upon the march without any loss of time by stretching lines from front to rear upon the outside of loaded waggons, and suspending the meat upon them, where it is allowed to remain until sufficiently cured to be packed away. Salt is never used in this process, and is not required, as the meat, if kept dry, rarely putrefies.

Marcy

We first ate the flesh of a snake at Graham's Town, South Africa. A friend had brought us a puff-adder as a specimen; and, when we had skinned it, the flesh looked so white and firm that we cut out a junk, about six inches long, and as thick as our wrist, and desired the Kafir girl, who acted as cook, to fry it. An acquaintance who partook of it acknowledged that it was good, and that only the thought of eating snake prevented his enjoying it more fully.

Lord & Baines

We had no salt, sugar, coffee, or tobacco, which, at a time when men are performing the severest labour that the human system is capable of enduring, was a great privation. In this destitute condition we found a substitute for tobacco in the bark of the red willow, which grows upon many of the mountain streams in that vicinity. The outer bark is first removed with a knife, after which the inner bark is scraped up into ridges around the sticks, and held in the fire until it is thoroughly roasted, when it is taken off the stick, pulverised in the hand, and is ready for smoking. It has the narcotic properties of the tobacco, and is quite agreeable to the taste and smell. The sumach leaf is also used by the Indians in the same way, and has a similar taste to the willow bark. A decoction of the dried wild or horse mint, which we found abundant under the snow, was quite palatable, and answered instead of coffee. It dries up in that climate, but does not lose its flavour. We suffered greatly for the want of salt; but, by burning the outside of our mule steaks, and sprinkling a little gunpowder upon them, it did not require a very extensive stretch of the imagination to fancy the presence of both salt and pepper.

Marcy

Our journeys have taught us the wisdom of the Esquimaux appetite, and there are few among us who do not relish a slice of raw blubber, or a chunk of frozen walrus beef. The liver of a walrus (Awuktanuk) eaten with little slices of his fat, of a verity is a delicious morsel. Fire would ruin the curt pithy expression of vitality which belongs to its uncooked pieces. Charles Lamb's roast pig was nothing to Awuktanuk. I wonder that raw beef is not eaten at home. Deprived of extraneous fibre, it is neither indigestible nor difficult to masticate. With acids and condiments it makes a salad which an educated palate cannot help relishing; and as a powerful and condensed heat-making and antiscorbutic food it has no rival. I make this last broad assertion after carefully testing it truth. The natives of South Greenland prepare themselves for a long journey in the cold by a course of frozen seal. At Upernavik they do the same with the narwhal, which is thought more heat making than the seal, while the bear, to use their own expression, is "stronger travel" than all. In the far north, where the explorer has to carefully husband such food as good fortune may cast in his way, no portion of an animal is wasted.

Elisha Kent Kane, M.D.
'Arctic Explorations', 1853

A BATTLE WITH THE KING OF THE FROZEN SEAS.

Flesh from Live Animals. — The truth of Bruce's well-known tale of the Abyssinians and others occasionally slicing out a piece of a live ox for food is sufficiently confirmed. Thus Dr. Beke observes, "There could be no doubt of the fact. He had questioned hundreds of natives on the subject, and though at first they positively declared the statement to be a lie, many, on being more closely questioned, admitted the possibility of its truth, for they could not deny that cattle are frequently attacked by hyænas, whose practice is to leap on the animals from behind and at once begin devouring the hind quarters; and yet, if driven off in time, the cattle have still lived." — *Times,* Jan. 16, 1867.

It is reasonable enough that a small worn-out party should adopt this plan, when they are travelling in a desert where the absence of water makes it impossible to delay, and when they are sinking for want of food. If the ox were killed outright there would be material for one meal only, because a worn-out party would be incapable of carrying a load of flesh. By the Abyssinian plan the wounded beast continues to travel with the party, carrying his carcase that is destined to be turned into butcher's meat for their use at a further stage. Of course the idea is very revolting, for the animal must suffer as much as the average of the tens or hundreds of wounded hares and pheasants that are always left among the bushes after an ordinary English battue. To be sure, the Abyssinian plan should only be adopted to save human life.

When I travelled in South-West Africa, at one part of my journey a plague of bush-ticks attacked the roots of my oxen's tails. Their bites made festering sores, which ended in some of the tails dropping bodily off. I heard such accidents were not at all uncommon. The animals did not travel the worse for it. Now ox-tail soup is proverbially nutritious.

Galton

Foreign Food

Travellers *on the Continent* may live at a much cheaper rate, and also more comfortably, at a *"Table d'Hôte,"* or at a *"Restaurateur's,"* than if they are served in their own Apartment.

Choose such Foods as you have found that your Stomach can digest easily — Nutritive, but not of a Heating nature, and so plainly dressed, that they cannot be adulterated: *the Safest Foods* are Eggs, plain boiled or roasted Meat, and Fruit:— touch not any of those Queer Compounds commonly ycleped *Ragouts, Made Dishes, Puddings, Pies, &c.*

Above all, be on your guard against *Soup* and *Wine.* — Instead of Wine, it will often be better to drink Water, with the addition of one-eighth part of Brandy, which Travellers may carry with them. — *"The Oracle"* declares, that if A Man is not a very fastidious Epicure, he need never fear Hunger or Languor, when he can get good Bread and Water — *i.e.* provided he carry with him a Brunswick Sausage and a Bottle of Brandy.

Kitchiner

One meal a day is, in this climate, sufficient; and that ought to be after the work of the day is over; or, if made in the forenoon, a refreshing and digesting sleep ought to intervene between it and exertion. Turkish made-dishes are tempting, but fat, sheep roasted whole are dangerous viands with a traveller's appetite; and a general predominance of salt among the Albanians is intended to give the forbidden juice a stronger zest: against this, the prudent traveller ought to be on his guard; he would do well, if that were practicable, to confine himself to pilaf, yaoort (a species of sour milk), and eggs, which he can find every where: the first two form together a light, nutritive, and not unpalatable dish.

D. Urquhart:
'The Spirit of the East', 1838

Japanese food is of wide range and amazing variety. It is as much the delight of the native — whose tastes are catholic, and who regards the Nipponese cookery as the best extant, — as it is the despair of the foreigner, who considers most of it mawkish and unsatisfying. He fails signally to thrive long upon it.

Terry:
Japan

I arrived for the night at a hut, where there were fowls, and I begged the woman to cook one of them immediately.

As soon as the water in a large pot had boiled, the woman caught a hen, and killed it by firmly holding the head in her hand, while she gave the bird two or three turns in the air. To my horror and utter astonishment, she instantly put the fowl into the pot, feathers and all; and although I had resolved to rough it on my journey, yet I positively could not make up my mind to drink such broth or "potage au naturel" as I thought she was preparing for me. I ran to her, and, in very bad Spanish, loudly protested against her cookery; however, she quietly explained to me that she had only put the fowl there to scald it, and as soon as I let go her arm she took it out. The feathers all came off together, but they stuck to her fingers almost as fast as they had before to the fowl. After washing her hands, she took a knife, and very neatly cut off the wings, the two legs, the breast and the back, which she put one after another into a small pot with some beef suet and water, and the rest of the fowl she threw away.

Captain F. B. Head:
'Rough Notes Taken During Some Rapid Journeys Across the Pampas and among the Andes', 1828

In Canton . . . dried rats have a recognized place in the poulterers' shops, and find a ready market, not only among those who have a taste for them, but also among people who have a tendency to baldness, the flesh of rats being considered an effectual "hair-restorer".

Robert K. Douglas:
'China', 1887

In Dominica and the French islands the edible frog known as the crapaud (*Rana esculenta*) is considered a great delicacy, and one might add, very succulent. It is served to unsuspecting visitors under the name of "mountain chicken".

Aspinall:
West Indies

Turtle Stew —

It was in one large wooden bowl, round which sat about twenty convives. My own black servant sat next to me, and every one dipped his hand, armed with a piece of bread, into the same dish. At the time of my voyage to Jeddah this sort of communism in feeding was rather extraordinary to me; but since that time I have for years been in the constant habit of "dipping my finger in the dish" with niggers, and think even now that that mode of eating is far more convenient and, as it is practised in the East, quite as cleanly as the use of knives and forks; and, after all, "fingers were made first".

Parkyns:
Abyssinia

In almost all country places out of England it is impossible to avoid the greasy dishes which are apparently preferred by all except our own countrymen; and a frequent consequence is rancid indigestion, with nauseous taste in the mouth, and flatulence or diarrhœa. A few drops of vinegar or lemon-juice and a little cayenne pepper in the plate are the readiest correctives.

Another article of cuisine that offends the bowels of unused Britons is garlic. Not uncommonly in southern climes an egg with the shell on is the only procurable animal food without garlic in it. Flatulence and looseness are the frequent results. Bouilli, with its accompaniments of mustard sauce and water melon, is the safest resource, and not an unpleasant one, after a little education.

Chambers

Now that we have fallen on the subject of national tastes, we must not forget to describe the most atrocious compound ever presented to man in the shape of food. It is the Russian soup called *Batinia,* which, to English palates, tastes worse than poison, but which these our allies, high and low of them, delight in as the greatest delicacy on earth. Hearing so much in its praise, we ventured once, and only once — for there is no fear of its being asked for a second time — to give a hint that we should like to make a trial of it. But — *"O dura Russorum ilia!"* — the taste is not yet away from our lips, nor are we yet persuaded that the skin has returned to our throats.

A plateful of this yellow liquid — it ought not to be called soup — was placed before us, with a scum on its top something like a thin coating of sulphur.

Adventurously diving through this surface, what did we discover? — Lumps of rotten sturgeon, slices of bitter cucumber, spoonfuls of biting mustard; in short a concatenation of all the most putrid, most acrid, most villanous substances that nature produces. The Witches' broth was nothing to it:—

> "Eye of newt, and toe of frog,
> Wing of bat, and tongue of dog,"

would be delicacies most exquisite, compared with these Russian horrors. But, though both *smell* and *sight* were well-nigh daunted, we resolved to persevere like men. We had begun the perilous adventure, and could not with honour draw back, before *taste* had also been put to proof. A spoonful of it was accordingly raised to the lips; when, lo! besides its other recommendations, it was found to be literally as cold as ice: for the mountain projecting above the surface, which we had innocently supposed to be some nice redeeming jelly, of Russian invention, turned out to be a lump of ice from "the frosty Caucasus," or some other vile place. That mouthful was the worst we ever swallowed! It would be impossible to depict the looks of anguish which we, a party of deluded, inexperienced Englishmen, cast on each other. It took away the breath; tears rolled from our eyes; we were more than satisfied — we were humbled, silenced, overcome; and made a vow before the whole company of strangers, never more to be lured into an attempt to make new discoveries in the adventurous region of Russian dishes.

Bremner:

On the walls of the dining-room there are bills of fare. The following is a translation of one:—

Cat's flesh, one basin	10 cents
Black cat's flesh, one small basin	5 cents
Wine, one bottle	3 cents
Wine, one small bottle	1½ cents
Congee	2 cash
Ketchup, one basin	3 cash
Black dog's grease, one tael	4 cents
Black cat's eyes, one pair	4 cents

All guests dining at this restaurant are requested to be punctual in their payments.

Robert K. Douglas:
'China', 1887.

Recipes

Although the flesh of the elephant is extremely coarse, the foot and trunk are excellent, if properly cooked. A hole should be dug in the earth, about four feet deep, and two feet six inches in diameter, the sides of which should be perpendicular; in this a large fire should be lighted, and kept burning for four or five hours with a continual supply of wood, so that the walls become red-hot. At the expiration of the blaze, the foot should be laid upon the glowing embers, and the hole should be covered closely with thick pieces of green wood laid parallel together to form a ceiling; this should be covered with wet grass, and the whole should be plastered with mud, and stamped tightly down to retain the heat. Upon the mud, a quantity of earth should be heaped, and the oven should not be opened for thirty hours, or more. At the expiration of that time, the foot will be perfectly baked, and the sole will separate like a shoe, and expose a delicate substance that, with a little oil and vinegar, together with an allowance of pepper and salt, is a delicious dish that will feed about fifty men.

Baker:
Abyssinia

THE FIGHT WITH

Very few like biscuits at sea; but of course you will be necessitated to take a few. There is one way I have seen them made into a nice dish. Steep a few in cold water for three or four minutes; take them out, and fry them with a small quantity of lard or butter and salt, in a frying-pan; some are very fond of them done this way.

General Hints to Emigrants, 1866

A mode of cooking a dish of hippopotamus, discovered by Sir Samuel Baker, is well worth bearing in mind. Speaking of it, he says: "I tried boiling the fat flesh and skin together, the result being that the skin assumed the appearance of the green fat of the turtle, but is far superior. A piece of the head thus boiled, and then soused in vinegar, with chopped onions and cayenne pepper and salt, throws brawn completely into the shade."

Lord & Baines

THE HIPPOPOTAMUS.

The first thing to be done was to prepare the bread, for we were all hungry: and now, while I describe the way in which it was made, my readers should lend their attention, and, if found agreeable, make note of it; for it may happen that at a picnic some fair lady may have a longing for fresh bread, and if you are gallant you may, by this recipe, present it to her in a very short time, hot and smoking from the fire. First, you must of course have flour, of which you take a sufficient quantity: this you mix with water to make a stiff dough, which you knead up well with your hands into balls, each the size and form of a nine-pound shot. Then take a round pebble, heated previously in the fire, and making a hole in your loaf, poke it in and close the mouth: then, putting the loaf on the embers, you must be careful to turn it about, so that it may not be done more on one side than the other. In about ten minutes it will be baked and ready for eating: so that you will, if hungry and clever, have made, baked, and eaten your bread in not much more than a quarter of an hour, which all will allow to be sufficiently quick. The only fault to find with bread thus made is, that seldom more than the outside and inside surfaces are at all baked.

Having thus dined, with no sauce but a good appetite, we reposed for an hour or so till the great heat had abated. Some people may think that bread and water is a hard diet on a journey, but they are much mistaken. A man who knows how to appreciate bread and water may with that simple diet go more comfortably through a hard day's march in a hot climate than if attended by the best cook in England with all his *batterie de cuisine*; and for this plain reason, that though the culinary art may procure him some enjoyment at the half-way halt, yet he will find that such temporary pleasure must be severely paid for in the afternoon's walk; meats and all other strong food being of too heating a nature. But, if hungry, don't eat your bread greedily, and then wash it down with buckets of water to prevent choking; sop your bread in the water, and then eat it; you will thus at once appease your hunger and quench your thirst, without being in danger of strangulation, or of having to carry a few extra pounds weight of water rattling about in your stomach for the remainder of the day; above all things, make it an invariable rule *always to drink as little water as possible,* remembering that the more you drink the more you will thirst.

Parkyns:
Abyssinia

In Tartary it is said to be common for a rider to cut a thin steak of beef and lay it under his saddle before he sets out on his journey, and after some hours he finds that the combined effects of constant pressure and warmth have, if not cooked it, at least rendered it palatable enough to be eaten.

Lord & Baines

Drink

Water for drinking ought to be invariably carried in glass bottles as it acquires a taste (or delicate palates fancy that it does) from the leathern bottles of the country.

Hints to Overland Travellers (From India — via Egypt) 1838

Digging Wells.— In default of spades, water is to be dug for with a sharp-pointed stick. Take it in both hands, and, holding it upright like a dagger, stab and dig it in the ground, as in fig. 1; then clear out the loose earth with the hand, as in fig. 2. Continue thus working with the stick and hand alternately, and a hole as deep as the arm is easily made.

Galton

Many persons have attributed their escape from the severe malarial fevers of the Danube, to the use of porter as their common beverage . . .

Brandy is very useful in marshy situations, but should be used with moderation.

Murray:
The Ionian Islands, Greece, Turkey, Asia Minor, and Constantinople, 1840.

Avoid native drinks, as they will probably have been diluted with dirty water, or prepared in unclean vessels.

William Henry Crosse, M.D.:
Medical Hints, 1906

The heat increases one's thirst by producing perspiration, and the only remedy to this is tea, for there is nothing so effectual in allaying thirst. It will often be found useful to carry a bottle of cold tea. Old travellers frequently carry in their holsters, instead of pistols, a small teapot, with a paper of tea, and another of sugar, on the one side, and a cup.

Murray:
Turkey in Asia, 1878

The national drink, called *quass,* as well as the national soups, *batvinia* and *shtshie* (cabbage soup), we earnestly recommend the traveller to avoid: the former is made of a pound of salt, two pounds of barley meal, and a pound and a half of honey, mixed together, and after having been heated in an oven is strained and left to cool; though not often met with at the tables of the rich in St. Petersburgh it is highly esteemed by all classes, and a Russian of the lower class can no more live without his quass than fish without water; moreover, it forms the foundation of his soups and sauces, for these are rarely made with unadulterated water. The stranger will understand, therefore, how necessary the foregoing caution is when he learns that batvinia, the summer soup, is not only composed of raw herbs, berries, chopped cucumbers, black bread, lumps of ice, and cold fish, but that the whole of these ingredients swim in cold quass. We remember when that Megatherium of critics, the *Quarterly Review,* did us the honour to notice our puny literary efforts, we were taunted for expressing our disapprobation of this compound, on the ground that some persons do not like olives, and others prefer stale and tainted oysters; but even at this distance of time we cannot see in this dish any evidence of a correct taste — if taste, like beauty, be an abstract thing. Women in Lapland console themselves after their accouchement with a glass of train oil — a glass of sherry is, we think, in better taste.

Murray:
Finland and Russia, 1849

The wine of the country in Greece is resinous and scarcely drinkable to a foreigner, savouring of sealing-wax and vinegar.

Murray:
The Ionian Islands, Greece, Turkey, Asia Minor, and Constantinople, 1840.

The Demon Drink

Persons addicted to alcoholic drinks are specially liable to Heat Fever, and in such the disease is apt to prove fatal.

The Travellers' Medical and Surgical Guide, 1888.

I would specially urge on [the traveller], if he is visiting the tropics, the absolute necessity of extreme moderation in the use of alcohol. Indeed, it is better to go to the extreme of abstaining altogether than to go to excess in this matter, which is remorselessly punished by nature. At the same time, alcohol is a valuable medicine and should not be excluded from the traveller's repertory. For an expedition not likely to last more than a year, the following amount will be found sufficient:— Two dozen of good champagne, three bottles of sherry, four bottles of brandy, and four of whisky. Claret, burgundy, and port travel badly, although as tonics and blood-making wines they are among the best . . . Except under extraordinary circumstances, such as accidents or deadly faintness, alcohol should never be taken in the day-time, but reserved for the evening, and if the want of it then felt, it should preferably be taken in the form of champagne, or brandy or whisky and water. The practice of so many German travellers of taking small quantities of neat brandy or other spirit in Africa is most deleterious, and if pursued for any length of time will inevitably prove fatal.

Johnston

With the single exception of the best brands of champagne, the writer is unable to recommend, beside pure whisky and brandy, any other form of alcoholic beverage for use in the tropics. Beer and porter, especially the stronger kinds, provoke liver derangements and claret of good quality can rarely be obtained by the traveller.

Douglas W. Freshfield & Capt. W. J. L. Wharton:
'Hints to Travellers', 1889. (Medical Hints — G. E. Dobson)

A consensus of opinion, taken from numbers of the medical men throughout the island, bears out the statement that fully one-half the deaths of visitors or temporary residents from febrile causes can readily be traced to excess in liquor, or those exposures which intoxication so generally leads to.

The Imperial Guide to India 1904.

Above all things, do not take your *decanters,* or your *cork-screw;* and resolve never to use either again. You are going to a country where claret used to be about eight English pence a bottle, and where you may literally swim in whisky or rum. But, resolve *never to taste either.* Drinking is the great vice of the country; and, if you wish to have health and happiness, you will rigidly abstain from that fatal and disgusting vice.

Cobbett

Observe the strictest temperance. Drop all thoughts of tonics, according to the rules of "west coasters", "old traders", "African travellers", or your own self-deceiving fancies. If you are in absolute need of a tonic apply to the doctor, or to the simple rule of never during daylight taking more than one ounce of any liquor or wine. Your best tonic would be two grams of quinine as compressed in Tablets by Burroughs and Wellcome, of Snow Hill Buildings, London.

Henry M. Stanley:
'The Congo Free State', 1885.

No. 290. 'TABLOID' Brand MEDICINE CHEST. Made of japanned sheet iron. Outside measurements, 15¼ x 12½ x 8¼. Weight of chest when fitted, about 40 lb.

Medical Advice

"CONGO" MEDICINE CHEST

Strong Metal, containing forty 2-ounce bottles, in moveable wooden tray with covers; fitted with partitions for instruments, etc. Size: 16 by 11 by 9in. PRICE—Without medicines 50/. With compressed and other medicines, instruments and "Travellers' Medical Guide," etc., according to list, £7 to £20. Weight of Chest about 40 lbs.

The "Congo" Medicine Chest is also supplied in either leather or teak-wood as may be desired.

Emetics. — For want of proper physic, drink a charge of gunpowder in a tumblerful of warm water or soap-suds, and tickle the throat.

Galton

It used to be said that the best way to ensure good health was to keep the pores of the skin open and the mouth shut!

Aspinall:
West Indies.

Plethoric persons, and those who are subject to a spitting of Blood, and indeed all Valetudinarians, should consult their Medical Adviser before they undertake a long Journey.

Those who are afflicted with a Rupture, should take a spare Truss with them — this advice applies to a much greater number of persons than may be supposed — "after a minute investigation of the number of Ruptured people in this kingdom, male and female, I am induced to take them upon an average of *one* to *fifteen.*" — *Turnbull on Ruptures,* 12mo. 1798, p. 4.

This complaint is brought on by many causes, which people are more exposed to abroad than they are at Home:— great Fatigue — Exertion in carrying weights beyond their strength — violent Coughing — Laughing — Leaping — Falls, &c. All persons who are afflicted with a Rupture, should remember that any sudden exertion or violent motion may produce the most alarming consequences.

Kitchiner

As a general rule, abstinence does no harm in these climates, but, on the contrary, it is always a good thing, and often necessary. I never felt lighter in my life, or more free from the many ills that vex humanity, than during this my long period of semi-starvation. Wounds of all kinds healed on me like magic, and I never knew what it was to feel lazy or fatigued. On one or two occasions I remember being much astonished at the little I suffered from otherwise ugly wounds about the feet. Once, in running down the stony and almost precipitous path which leads to the Mareb, I struck my bare foot against an edge of rock, which was as sharp as a razor, and a bit of flesh, with the whole of the nail of my left foot little toe, was cut off, leaving only the roots of the nail. This latter I suppose to have been the case, as it has grown all right again. I could not stop longer than to polish off the bit which was hanging by a skin, for we were in chase of a party of Barea, who had cut the throats of three of Waddy Hil's nephews the night before — (by the way I'll tell that story afterwards, to show what cowardly louts some of the Abyssinians are) — but was obliged to go on running for about twenty miles that afternoon, the greater part of the way up to our ankles in burning sand. Whether this cured it I know not, but I scarcely suffered at all from it next day, and forgot it the day after.

Parkyns: Abyssinia

Treatment for Fever

Sometimes violent exertion, producing perspiration and exhaustion, if practised in time, may avert an attack. We have heard of a doctor visiting a man when the shivering fit was about to come on, who locked the door, mixed two glasses of stiff hot grog, put on the gloves, and engaged his patient in a boxing match, which, at least, for that time averted the fever.

Lord & Baines

Intermittent Fever — The first indication is to get a *free* action of the bowels; give two "Livingstone's Rousers"* at once.

*(Six grams each of Jalap and Rhubarb, with four grains of Calomel, and the same quantity of Quinine).

The Travellers' Medical and Surgical Guide, 1888.

"LIVINGSTONE" MEDICINE CHEST.

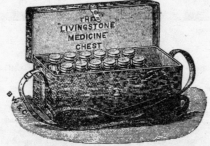

Raw Hide, containing twelve 4 oz. bottles. Fitted with leather strap for convenience of carrying. Very suitable for missionaries and travellers. Size : 11 by 7 by 4 inches. Price—Empty, 30/-. Fitted with medicines, instruments, and "Guide," from £4. A smaller size, containing 2-oz. bottles, empty 25/-, fitted from £3.

Treatment for Diarrhoea

The following is a good mode of treatment for diarrhoea, or even for the beginning of suspected dysentery. First take an emetic of ipecacuanha, and in the morning a mild aperient, as 15 grs. of rhubarb with 2 grs. of calomel; on the following day, 2 grs. of ipecacuanha with ¼ gr. of opium morning and evening, nothing being eaten but boiled rice, sweetened with white sugar. But if this does not stop the complaint, and tenesmus gives the well-known sign of decided dysentery, a dose of 20 grs. of calomel with ¼ gr. of opium, should be taken, which must be followed next morning by a dose of castor oil. This generally cuts the matter short; but it is as well to follow it up with 2 grs. of ipecacuanha and ½ gr. of opium three or four times within the 12 or 24 hours, for two or three days after. In severe cases, an injection of nitrate of silver (caustic) has been employed with great success; but this can only be done under medical advice.

Murray:
Egypt, 1847

The change of Food and Drink occasionally gives rise to a morbid acidity in the Stomach, &c. and to a very distressing Diarrhoea: the remedy for this is,

Compound Powder of Kino, one drachm;
Compound Powder of Chalk, half an ounce.
Mix thoroughly together, and divide it into Six Powders, One of which may be taken once or twice a day, in a teaspoonful of Brandy and three tablespoonsful of Water.

This conveniently portable Astringent will keep good for Years in any Climate.

Kitchiner

As a safeguard against accidental diarrhœa it is wise to be prepared with some chalk and opium powders (*Pulvis Cretae aromaticus cum Opio. Pharm. Brit.*) made up in 20-grain packets, in thin gutta-percha or oil silk, to keep them dry. In northerly latitudes half a packet, namely, ¼ grm of opium, can be taken after each relaxation. But in warm countries a more efficient, at least a more permanently efficient remedy is to be found in lemon-juice. The patient should lie down flat, and keep sipping a mixture of half and half lemon juice and water, or simply sucking lemons, till the symptoms have ceased. The nausea and narcotism induced by opium are thus avoided, and there is no danger in taking an excess of the fruit. It is a good thing to get accustomed to the acidity of the flavour, for there is nothing so wholesome and convenient as a drink.

Chambers

If the diarrhœa comes on suddenly, the bowels should be cleared of all irritating matters by a laxative, such as a tablespoonful of castor oil and lemon juice . . . Afterwards, if still persistent, a mild opiate and astringent, *to simply check* (not "bind") the bowels will be of service. Such a combination is Lead and Opium.

Chronic Diarrhœa — *A recumbent position largely maintained* goes far toward alleviating and cutting short this disease.

The Travellers' Medical and Surgical Guide, 1888.

Treatment for Constipation.

Habitual constipation is a complaint to which Europeans are frequently subject after their arrival in India and arises as much from want of exercise as from any other cause. Medicine will prove far less effectual to remedy it, than a well regulated system of diet and regimen. Good active walking exercise, the use of bran bread, fruits, and plenty of good fresh drinking water will, if persevered with, probably effect all the good desired.

The so-called hydropathic treatment is most beneficial in these cases. The patient should sit in a small quantity of cold water every morning, for about a quarter of an hour, at the same time rubbing the abdomen gently with the hand or sponging it with cold water; or a wineglassful of cold water may be injected into the bowels, and retained there while a brisk walk is being taken. A wet bandage round the abdomen is also sometimes of the greatest benefit, and the mode of applying it is as follows:— Soak a double piece of American drill, twelve inches square in cold water; place this over the stomach, covering it with waterproof sheeting one inch larger all round than the wet cloth; and then apply a dry bandage round the body, fastening it with tape, or buckles and straps.

This should be applied early in the morning, and kept on for about two hours, during which time active exercise ought to be taken, and one or two tumblers of fresh water drunk, with or without some simple fruit, as the plantain or mango.

R. S. Mair, M.D.:
'Medical Guide for Anglo-Indians', 1878

Many persons become Costive when they travel, who are not at all so at Home — the change of Air, of Food and Drink, and the general change of Habits, very often produce this to an extremely inconvenient degree; therefore, every one should carry such Aperient Medicine as experience has convinced him suits his constitution, and will gently but effectually counteract the disposition we have mentioned.

Ponder well on the following sentence:— "APERIENT MEDICINE does *Enough,* if it accelerates or increases the customary Evacuation, and does *Too Much,* if it does more than occasion One, or at most, Two additional motions:— Bowels which are forced into double action to-day, must consequently become Costive to-morrow, and Constipation will be caused by the remedy you have recourse to, to remove it; and thus, one dose creates a necessity for another, till the poor Patient wants Physic almost as often as he wants Food."

Kitchiner

To Make Forty of Dr. Kitchiner's Peristaltic Persuaders.
Take Rhubarb finely pulverized, Two drachms;
Syrup (by weight) One drachm;
Oil of Carraway, Ten drops (Minims).
Make Forty Pills, each of which will contain Three
grains of Rhubarb.

At any time when your Stomach feels as if something is offending it, and it seems to say to your Mouth, "I wish You would be so obliging as to swallow something that will accelerate the Alvine exoneration," introduce two or three of these Pills — Experience will soon teach you the number convenient.

Peristaltic Persuaders are the most convenient Laxative for Travellers; but in the case of any thing extremely disagreeing with the Stomach, and a quick acting remedy be required, dissolve a teaspoonful of *Epsom* or *Glauber* Salts in half-a-pint of as warm water as you can drink, and repeat it every half-hour till it operates. Glauber's Salt keeps best in a warm Climate. Epsom Salt attracts moisture, is apt to deliquesce, and is preserved with more difficulty.

Kitchiner

THE SOCIETY OF APOTHECARIES OF LONDON.

MANUFACTURERS OF ALL PHARMACEUTICAL

PREPARATIONS OF THE HIGHEST QUALITY

PURE DRUGS AND CHEMICALS, AND SURGICAL APPLIANCES

APOTHECARIES' HALL,
LONDON. E.C.

Treatment for Sunstroke

Removal to the shade, a strictly recumbent posture, the administration of whisky or wine, or black coffee in small quantities by the mouth if the patient can swallow, or diluted two thirds and thrown into the rectum by syringe, will accomplish restoration in a short time. The hypodermic injection of half to one teaspoonful of whisky and water, equal parts, once in fifteen minutes till the patient is able to swallow, may prove more convenient.

The Travellers' Medical and Surgical Guide, 1888.

Let none, therefore, flatter themselves, although they may appear to have escaped any immediate ill effects from undue exposure to the sun, that it necessarily follows they have "got off" scatheless. A person may escape a sun-stroke or a fever, but who shall say when the seeds of disease may have been deposited in the liver, or how much more he may have increased his *predisposition* to suffer penalty on the next occasion? Prevention is better than cure; and surely every sensible person should avail himself of the former alternative, when only a trifling amount of care is required. What an amount of after-regret might have often been avoided, for some honourable and promising career cut short prematurely, had a little care and forethought been exercised in reference to this subject!

Hull:
India

Treatment for Sunburn

Owing to exposure to the sun while working at the Fish River drift on the preceding days, and also to having discarded coat, waistcoat, and neckcloth since leaving Grahamstown, my arms, neck, and shoulders were much swollen, and severely burnt and blistered, causing me much pain, and at night preventing me from sleeping. The kind-hearted noë, or lady of the farm, commiserating my condition, and wishing to alleviate my pain, informed me that she had an excellent recipe for sunburn, which she had often successfully administered to her husband and sons. One of the chief ingredients of the promised balsam was green tea, which was to be reduced to powder, of which she directed me to send her a little by one of my servants. I do not know what the other components might have been, but I well know that, on applying the ointment to the raw and swollen parts, it stung me as though it had been a mixture of salt and vinegar, giving me intense pain, and causing me to hop and dance about like one demented, and wish the Boer noë and her ointment in the realms of Pluto, to the infinite delight and merriment of my sympathising Hottentots.

Cumming:
South Africa

Treatment for Coorash

The plague of boils broke out, and every one was attacked more or less severely. Then came a plague of which Moses must have been ignorant, or he would surely have inflicted it upon Pharaoh. This was a species of itch, which affected all ages and both sexes equally; it attacked all parts of the body, but principally the extremities. The irritation was beyond description; small vesicles rose above the skin, containing a watery fluid, which, upon bursting, appeared to spread the disease. The Arabs had no control over this malady, which they called "coorash", and the whole country was scratching. The popular belief attributed the disease to the water of the Atbara at this particular season; although a horrible plague, I do not believe it to have any connexion with the well-known itch or "scabies" of Europe.

I adopted a remedy that I had found a specific for mange in dogs, and this treatment became equally successful in cases of coorash. Gunpowder, with the addition of one fourth of sulphur, made into a soft paste with water, and then formed into an ointment with fat: this should be rubbed over the whole body. The effect upon a black man is that of a well-cleaned boot — upon a white man it is still more striking; but it quickly cures the malady.

Baker:
Abyssinia

"COLONIAL" MEDICINE CHEST.
(ORNAMENTED METAL OR TEAK WOOD).

Missionaries' Teak-wood Medicine Chest.

Furnished Complete, 70s.
For Stations and Expeditions.

This is especially designed for emergencies and family use. Besides being furnished with 16 one-and-a-half ounce bottles, and 4 three-quarter ounce bottles containing compressed and other drugs—those most commonly required by physicians and families—it has surgeons' bandages, scissors, lancet, needles and silk, adhesive, court, and mustard plasters, catheter, absorbent cotton, wound pad, etc. For physicians, missionaries, travellers, explorers, and use on board ship, these chests will be found to fill many an important want. PRICE— Fitted complete with leather strap for convenience of carrying, glass bottles, 50/-, tin bottles 70/-. Chest and bottles only, 10/-.

NOTE.—All the Medicine Cases and Chests can be fitted with Tabloids of compressed drugs, etc., according to order. Any of the above may be ordered of Burroughs, Wellcome & Co., Snow Hill Buildings, London, or through any chemist or wholesale druggist.

Treatment for Boils

Boils are sometimes very troublesome to equestrians. A small piece of nitrate of silver ought to be carried in the baggage, and on the first tenderness, redness, and hardness the part should be damped and the caustic lightly crossed twice over it. The object is not to make the cuticle rise in a blister, but to contract and render insensitive the cutis. The pressure of the tightened skin causes the boil to die away.

Chambers

Treatment for Blisters

It not unfrequently happens that the feet of those not thoroughly accustomed to hard tramping will become blistered. When the eggs of either poultry or wild birds are to be obtained, it is a good plan to break one or two, according to their size, into each shoe before starting in the morning.

Lord & Baines

To prevent the feet from blistering during a protracted walking tour, they may be rubbed morning and evening with brandy and tallow. A warm footbath with bran will be found soothing after a long day's march. Soaping the inside of the stocking is another well-known safeguard against abrasion of the skin.

Baedecker:
The Eastern Alps, 1883.

Rub the Feet at going to Bed with Spirits mixed with Tallow dropped from a lighted Candle into the palm of the hand. On the following morning no blister will exist. The Spirits seem to possess the healing power, the Tallow serving only to keep the skin soft and pliant. The Soles of the Feet, the Ancles, and Insteps, should be rubbed well; and even when no blisters exist, the application may be useful as a preventive: and while on this head, I would recommend foot travellers never to wear right and left Shoes — it is bad economy, and indeed serves to cramp the feet.

John Dundas Cochrane:
'Narrative of a Pedestrian Journey Through Russia and Siberian Tartary', 1824

Treatment for Snake Bites

Apply at once a ligature, or ligatures, at intervals of a few inches, as tight as you can possibly tie them, and tighten the one nearest to the wound by twisting it with a stick or other such agent. Scarify the wound and let it bleed freely. Apply either a hot iron or live coal, or explode some gunpowder on the part: and apply either carbolic acid or some mineral acid or caustic. Let the patient suck the wound whilst you are getting the cautery ready, or, if anyone else will run the risk, let him do it. "If the bite be on a toe or finger, especially if the snake have been recognised as a deadly one, either completely excise, or immediately amputate at the next joint. If the bite be on another part, where a ligature cannot be applied, or indeed if it be on the limbs above the toe or fingers, cut the part out at once completely. Let the patient be quiet."

Sir J. Fayrer, M.D., F.R.S., Late Nineteenth Century.

Rattlesnake Bites

Upon the southern routes to California rattlesnakes are often met with, but it is seldom that any person is bitten by them; yet this is a possible contingency, and it can never be amiss to have an antidote at hand.

Hartshorn applied externally to the wound, and drunk in small quantities diluted with water whenever the patient becomes faint or exhausted from the effects of the poison, is one of the most common remedies.

In the absence of all medicines, a string or ligature should at once be bound firmly above the puncture, then scarify deeply with a knife, suck out the poison, and spit out the saliva.

Andersson, in his book on South-western Africa, says: "In the Cape Colony the Dutch farmers resort to a cruel but apparently effective plan to counteract the bad effects of a serpent's bite. An incision having been made in the breast of a living fowl, the

bitten part is applied to the wound. If the poison be very deadly, the bird soon evinces symptoms of distress, becomes drowsy, droops its head, and dies. It is replaced by a second, a third, and more if requisite. When, however, the bird no longer exhibits any of the signs just mentioned, the patient is considered out of danger. A frog similarly applied is supposed to be equally efficacious."

Haunberg, in his *Travels in South Africa*, mentions an antidote against the bite of serpents. He says: "The blood of the turtle was much cried up, which, on account of this extraordinary virtue, the inhabitants dry in the form of small scales or membranes, and carry about them when they travel in this country, which swarms with this most noxious vermin. Whenever any one is wounded by a serpent, he takes a couple of pinches of the dried blood internally, and applies a little of it to the

91

wound." . . .

I knew of another instance near Fort Towson, in Northern Texas, where a small child was left upon the earthen floor of a cabin while its mother was washing at a spring near by. She heard a cry of distress, and, on going to the cabin, what was her horror on seeing a rattlesnake coiled around the child's arm, and striking it repeatedly with its fangs. After killing the snake, she hurried to her nearest neighbour, procured a bottle of brandy, and returned as soon as possible; but the poison had already so operated upon the arm that it was as black as a negro's. She poured down the child's throat a huge draught of the liquor, which soon took effect, making it very drunk, and stopped the action of the poison. Although the child was relieved, it remained sick for a long time, but ultimately recovered. . . .

A Delaware remedy, which is said to be efficacious, is to burn powder upon the wound, but I have never known it to be tried excepting upon a horse. In this case it was successful, or, at all events, the animal recovered.

Of all the remedies known to me, I should decidedly prefer ardent spirits. It is considered a sovereign antidote among our Western frontier settlers, and I would make use of it with great confidence. It must be taken until the patient becomes very much intoxicated, and this requires a large quantity, as the action of the poison seems to counteract its effects.

Marcy

Treatment for Sea-Sickness

The first great trial with which the majority . . . have to contend is sea-sickness. Many things have been recommended for the prevention of this, but none have been successful . . . A little bit of camphor chewed once a day will frequently act as a palliative, if not as a preventive; in this way also a drop or two of chloroform, or, better still, chloric ether, or of creosote, on a lump of sugar, will be useful.

General Hints to Emigrants, 1866

Sea-voyages have a powerful curative effect on some invalids, but they do not generally bring healthy persons into very good condition. If it is calm, landsmen over-eat themselves, take too little exercise, sleep badly, and get their bowels constipated. If it is rough, they suffer from sea-sickness and the badness of ventilation below.

The sea-sickness of short voyages may be considerably palliated by rational preparation, and pending the growth and schooling of that promising twin, the "Castalia," it is well worth while to try and palliate it. In the first place care should be taken to finish all preliminary arrangements as long before starting as you can, so that a day or two may be given to rest and a temperance somewhat more than usual. In case the eyes or skin are dingy and yellow, take a purge of aloes or taraxacum. Go on board in good time, so as to secure a comfortable post. During a short voyage if it is evidently going to be rough, go below and lie down immediately if possible. While you remain on deck, be very warmly clothed, and especially let no chill affect the abdomen or back. For a short time, drawing in a full breath and fixing the diaphragm during the sinking vertical motion of the ship, will keep off nausea, especially in the standing posture; the practice also assists you in getting your sea-legs; but it cannot be depended on for long. Should the stomach feel empty, and still more if any dry retching occurs, take bottled porter and biscuit spread with a little butter and cayenne pepper — which last article, by the way, amply repays the space it will occupy in a traveller's pocket throughout a journey, so useful is it on all occasions. Nutritious food should be taken when practicable, but loading the stomach with trash brings on sickness; though, truly enough, it facilitates the process of vomiting, and prevents the regurgitation of bile, which is always peculiarly painful after dry retching.

If the voyage be by night, and sufficiently long to make a night's rest of say seven or eight hours at least, it is worth while to swallow a full dose of chloral on embarking, and to sleep through one's trouble. But when you have to wake up in two or three hours to disembark, you feel ill all the next day, and perhaps longer.

Ice-bags, and all other specific "charms" for sea-sickness, have turned out mere trade puffs; and rational treatment, as above advised, remains the only hope for the landsman.

Chambers

We had *sea-sickness,* a plenty, for about ten days. While that is going on, certainly, the miserableness of the creatures cannot well be surpassed. While it lasts, you will hardly have any reflections at all: you will think, if you do think, that the world ought never to have been made, particularly the watery part of it. Some people, however, are never sea-sick at all. I never was but once, which I have always ascribed to abstinence from strong drink, and to my moderate eating, as well previous to the voyage as during it.

Cobbett

For sea-sickness there is no general specific, though some remedies are occasionally found very efficacious. Champagne, Moselle, or sparkling hock, are often found to have an excellent effect in settling the stomach; and a small case of pint or half-pint bottles of either, will probably, therefore, be found a valuable acquisition. A bottle or two of really good port or sherry will not be amiss in cases of subsequent prostration. All effervescing drinks are good in sea-sickness.

Hull:
India

The passenger at sea spends much of his life in the open air. Thus, his first appearance in the morning is for an airing on deck. For these purposes he will have judiciously supplied himself with a pair of slippers and also of pyjamas. These latter, thin flannel trousers (and jacket), are invaluable both for these daily purposes and in the tropics for that sleeping on deck which is often so pleasant and so health-giving. It is well to adopt the precaution of always sleeping in *flannel* garments. This is an absolute necessity if one would avoid cholera and other tropical illnesses. It is advisable to avoid sleeping in the direct rays of the moon. Neuralgia with various unpleasant results, such as contortions of the features, are often popularly attributed to the action of the moon's rays upon the sleeper's face.

W. S. Loftie:
Orient Line Guide, 1885

Hygiene

It is remarkable that, in most eastern countries, cleanliness makes a great part of their religion. The Mahomatan, as well as the Jewish religion, enjoins various bathings, washings, and purifications. No doubt these were designed to represent inward purity; but they are at the same time calculated for the preservation of health.

However whimsical these washings may appear to some, few things would seem more to prevent diseases than a proper attention to many of them.

Were every person, for example, after handling a dead body, visiting the sick, &c., to wash before he went into company, or sat down to meat, he would run less hazard, either of catching the infection himself, or communicating it to others.

Enquire Within Upon Everything, 1873.

Washing Oneself. — *Warmth of Dirt.* — There is no denying the fact, though it be not agreeable to confess it, that dirt and grease are great protectors of the skin against inclement weather, and that therefore the leader of a party should not be too exacting about the appearance of his less warmly-clad followers. Daily washing, if not followed by oiling, must be compensated by wearing clothes. Take the instance of a dog. He will sleep out under any bush, and thrive there, so long as he is not washed, groomed, and kept clean; but if he be, he must have a kennel to lie in. The same is the case with a horse; he catches cold if he is groomed in the day, and turned out at nights; but he never catches cold when left wholly to himself. A savage will never wash unless he can grease himself afterwards — grease takes the place of clothing to him. There must be a balance between the activity of the skin and the calls upon it; and where the exposure is greater, there must the pores be more defended. In Europe, we pass our lives in a strangely artificial state; our whole body swathed in many folds of dress, excepting the hands and face — the first of which are frequently gloved. We can afford to wash, but naked men cannot.

Galton

Washing cannot be properly done in the interior. One or two changes of underclothes and sheets should therefore be despatched . . . to different places on the route, and the dirty linen . . . sent home.

Satow & Hawes:
Japan

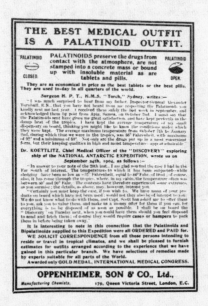

95

INNS — The first to arrive has the prior right to the hot bath.

Satow & Hawes:
Japan

The Fellah's notions of cleanliness are faint, in the extreme, and the traveller will do well to avoid a closer proximity, than is absolutely necessary.

Hints to Overland Travellers (from India — via Egypt), 1838

Treatment for Broken Bones

Lower Jaw.— The lower jaw must be fixed to the upper, by means of a bandage with four tails. This is made by taking a piece of roller bandage one yard and a quarter long and three inches wide; cutting a longitudinal slit at its centre, and one inch from the edge large enough to admit the chin; and tearing a slit down each end to within one inch and a half of the centre slit. The chin is now placed in the centre slit with the narrow edge beneath the lower lip, and the broad edge under the chin; the narrow upper tails are then carried straight backward, and firmly knotted behind at the upper part of the neck, and the broad lower tails carried upward, and tightly knotted on the top of the scalp. Lastly, all four tails are brought together at the back of the head and firmly tied. Occasionally this mode of treatment may be assisted by passing a piece of thin wire round the teeth on each side of the fracture. The patient should rinse his mouth out frequently with weak Condy's fluid and water or Hazeline.

Union usually takes place in about four weeks.

'The Traveller's Medical and Surgical Guide', 1888

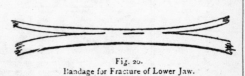

Fig. 20.
Bandage for Fracture of Lower Jaw.

Fig. 21.
Bandage for Fracture
of Lower Jaw.

The annexed illustration represents the mode of setting a dislocated shoulder. A man takes off his boot, sitting beside the patient, places his foot under the armpit, then taking hold of the wrist he pulls it steadily towards him, until the muscles relax and the bone slips into its place. A pad must then be secured under the armpit and the arm bound firmly to the side.

Lord & Baines

Treatment for Bleeding

Bleeding from the nose is arrested by making the patient lie on his back, raising the arms above the head, applying cold water to the nose, syringing out the nostril with hot or cold water, and by firmly plugging the outer opening of the nostril with rag or lint. If the blood still continues to trickle copiously down the throat, the inner opening of the nostril should also be plugged, by passing a gum-elastic catheter, with its wire removed, straight backwards — not upwards — along the nostril; when its end can be seen or felt at the back of the throat it must be hooked forward with the finger, and brought out at the mouth. A strong piece of string, having a firm roll of lint tightly tied at its centre, should now be attached to the end of the catheter, and the roll of lint drawn by the catheter and string into the inner or throat-opening of the nostril, and firmly wedged there. The roll of lint should be about 2½ inches in length, and rather thinner than the little finger; but its size must vary with the size of the opening. Lastly, both ends of the string, one hanging from the nose and the other from the mouth, should be loosely knotted together, and the outer opening of the nostril firmly plugged. The inner plug may be removed in twenty-four hours' time, and, if necessary, reinserted.

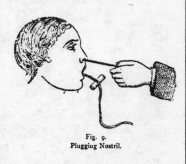

Fig. 9.
Plugging Nostril.

'The Traveller's Medical and Surgical Guide', 1888

VARIOUS MODES OF CARRYING

THE SICK OR WOUNDED

Carrying the Sick

Sometimes a man, though unable to walk, can sit and practically support himself; in this case two men may lay their muskets together, end for end, and hold them across between them for him to sit on, with his arms upon their shoulders; and even if they have no weapons at hand they may make him a very comfortable seat by joining their hands and arms, as shown in the above illustration.

Thus, the two bearers stand side by side, and half facing each other, No. 1 grasps his own right wrist with his left hand; No. 2 does the same; No. 1 then grasps the left wrist of No. 2 with his disengaged right hand, and this brings the right hand of No. 2 into the proper position to catch the left wrist of No. 1. In this easily extemporised chair they can bear a tolerably heavy man without undue strain on the muscles of their own arms; and when they become weary two others can at once take their places, or they may gain a little relief by interchanging the position of their right and left hands, while nothing can be more comfortable to a disabled man than the easy chair thus formed for him. Fig. 4. shows how a short pole can be used to form a seat-rest for carrying.

The mode of carrying used in mountainous countries by a chair strapped on the back of a porter, and still further secured by a band passing round his forehead, as shown at Fig. 5, might occasionally be found useful.

Lord & Baines

Mosquitoes

Every kind of vermin that exists to punish the nastiness and indolence of man, multiplies in the heat and dirt of Lisbon. From the worst and most offensive of these, cleanliness may preserve the English resident. The muskitoe is a more formidable enemy; if you read at night in summer, it is necessary to wear boots.

Robert Southey:
'Letters Written During a Journey in Spain', 1808.

Our mosquito preparations were as follows:

A flapper made of wood and leather: coffee-coloured net veils of circular cage form, passed over the hat and tucked in under the coat collar, having two hoops of whalebone to keep the nets from the features or neck . . .

A preparation of tar and oil in equal parts, for anointing the features unprotected by the veil. Carbolic acid and sweet oil, in the proportions of one to five, to neutralise the stings. A second dilution of alum with aromatic vinegar and glycerine, in the relative proportions of four, two, and one; lastly, strong aromatic vinegar and oil, this latter taken in the faint hope that by being disagreeable to the mosquito, we might be spared the last resource of tar. We had gauntlets reaching to our elbows, stiffened with whalebone — so stout that they would turn a sword cut and so huge that they stood out from our fingers farther than mosquito's proboscis could ever reach.

Edward Rae:
'The White Sea Peninsula', 1881.

There is no immediate cure for the irritation, often excessive, arising from a musquito bite; limejuice rubbed in does good in some cases, eau-de-Cologne in others, and arnica lotion in others; but the best plan is generally to leave them alone, and avoid scratching, which often leads to festered sores. If the itchiness and irritation is so great that it is impossible to abstain from scratching or rubbing, a brush ought to be used for this purpose, so as to avoid breaking the skin.

Hull:
India

My husband soon hit upon a very good expedient; he took me into one of the bed rooms, let down the musquito curtains, and beat out all the flies. He then emancipated me from my veil, I got into the bed, and he tucked the curtains securely round, leaving me in this *boudoir charmant* to spend the remainder of the day.

Mrs George Darby Griffith:
'A Journey Across the Desert', 1845

I will cite for the reader's benefit a recipe copied from one of the most worthy and popular English papers. The writer of it had suffered grievously from mosquito bites, and had hit upon the following remedy: Oil of pennyroyal, 2 dr.; oil of cedar, 2 dr.; glacial acetic acid, ½ dr.; pure carbolic acid, 1 dr.; camphor, 3 dr.; castor oil, 3 oz. He thinks this should be effectual. I should think so too. It ought to kill an elephant. The reader had better suspend his purchase of this preparation till I have completed certain chemical studies upon this subject. One of the chief ingredients I intend using is nitro-glycerine, and the preparation is to be called the Annihilator.

Edward Rae:
'The Country of the Moors,' 1877.

Lice

Before quitting Tchagen-Kouren we had bought in a chemist's shop a few sapeks' worth of mercury. We now made with it a prompt and specific remedy against the lice. We had formerly got this receipt from some Chinese, and as it may be useful to others, we think it right to describe it here. You take half-an-ounce of mercury, which you mix with old tea-leaves, previously reduced to paste by mastication. To render this softer, you generally add saliva, water would not have the same effect. You must afterwards bruise and stir it awhile, so that the mercury may be divided into little balls as fine as dust. You infuse this composition into a string of cotton, loosely twisted, which you hang round the neck; the lice are sure to bite at the bait, and they thereupon as surely swell, become red, and die forthwith. In China and in Tartary you have to renew this sanitary necklace once a month, for, otherwise, in these dirty countries you could not possibly keep clear from vermin, which swarm in every Chinese house and in every Mongol tent.

M. Huc:
'Travels in Tartary, Thibet and China' [Translated by W. Hazlitt], 1852

Fleas

To free empty houses of these insects, I have heard of resort being had to two curious expedients, which I may mention, but neither of which I can recommend:— (1) Putting a layer of straw over the whole floor of the house, and then setting it (the straw) alight; and (2) driving a herd of cattle through the building, to carry the fleas with them on their exit. In the first case, however, the house will probably be burned down, and in the second, damaged without any effectual remedy being obtained for the evil complained of.

Hull:
India

Shifts and Expedients
of Camp Life

CAMP SCENE IN AFRICA.

How to Render Shoes Waterproof

A pint of boiled Neatsfoot Oil;
Half a pound of Mutton Suet;
Six ounces of Bees Wax;
Four ounces of Resin.

These are to be melted together over a slow fire; and both the Upper leather and Soles of the Boots and Shoes, when quite New and Clean, are warmed and rubbed with this composition till the Leather is saturated.

Kitchiner

For use on the voyage, shoes or slippers are much more convenient than boots. The following is a cheap and excellent composition for preserving leather from the bad effects of sea-water:—

Lindseed oil, 1 gill; spirits of turpentine, 1 oz; bees wax, 1 oz; Burgundy pitch, ½ oz; to be well melted together and kept covered in a gallipot; lay on boots or shoes, rubbing it in well, and set them in a hot sun, or before the fire.

General Hints to Emigrants, 1866.

Matthew Lansberg, (the Francis Moore of the Continent), observes, in his last publication, that "if you wish to have a Shoe of durable materials, you should make the Upper leather of the mouth of a Hard-drinker; — for that never lets in Water."

Kitchiner

A simpler form of tent may be made at a moment's notice. If rain comes on, sit upright, joining the hands above the head as if you were about to dive, supporting the blanket on them, and allowing it to hang down on all sides that the rain may run off. If you have no blanket, you may still keep your gun, ammunition, or sketch-book dry by sitting on them.

Lord & Baines

TENT EXTEMPORISED FROM A BLANKET.

In South Africa, when the flats are swamped with heavy showers, and it would seem almost impossible to kindle the scanty fuel that can be obtained, the ant-hills with which the plain is covered prove the greatest imaginable boon to the traveller. One of these hills, 3ft. or 4ft. high, is selected, its top cut flat off, and a hole dug like an oven in its side. In this the fire is kindled, the flame rushes up through the galleries, the clay becomes red hot, and the kettle or frying-pan soon begins to feel its influence. But this is not all, for the galleries are most likely full of vegetable matter as well as of ants' eggs and larvæ, and these help to increase the flame. Of course it is cruel, but the traveller and his followers must have food.

Lord & Baines

The black fellow, being seated on the ground, holds down one end of the notched stick with each foot, fig. 2, and placing the point of the other stick into the notch, twirls it rapidly and forcibly between the palms of his hands. In doing this his hands gradually slip down the stick, and he has to shift them rapidly up again, which loses time: but two people, seated opposite, can alternately take up the rubbing, and more easily produce fire.

Galton

Fig. 2.

To those who wish to be entirely protected at night from intruders, I cannot do better than recommend a contrivance of Mr. Levinge's, which he imagined during his travels in the East, and which is equally adapted to a boat, a house, or a tent. It consists of a pair of sheets (*a*), about six feet long, sewed together at the bottom and the two sides, except where the piece (*c*) is attached to them, and by which you get in. To the upper end (*d*) is added a thin piece of muslin, serving as a mosquito net (*b*), which is drawn tight at the end by a tape or string, serving to suspend it to a nail (*f*). A short way from the end (at *e*) are fastened loops, through which a cane is threaded, to form a circle for distending the net. This cane is in three pieces, about three feet long, fitting into each other by sockets. After getting in by the opening of *c* you draw the tape tight to close its mouth, and tuck it in under the mattress, and you are secure from intruders, whether sleeping at night, or sitting under it by day.

Murray:
Egypt, 1847

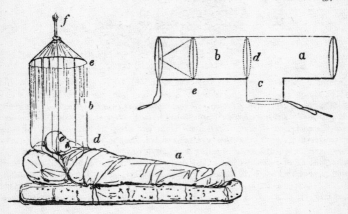

Travellers in countries where the atmosphere is very dry, as in the vicinity of the Mediterranean, sometimes lose their appetite for breakfast from want of sleep. This inconvenience may be overcome by soaking a sheet or some towels in water and spreading them out on the floor of the bedroom, so as to diffuse moisture through the air breathed during sleep.

Chambers

Preparing the Ground for a Bed. — Travellers should always root up the stones and sticks that might interfere with the smoothness of the place where they intend to sleep. This is a matter worth taking a great deal of pains about; the oldest campaigners are the most particular in making themselves comfortable at night. They should also scrape a hollow in the ground, of the shape shown in fig. 2, before spreading their sleeping-rugs. It is disagreeable enough to lie on a perfectly level surface, like that of a floor, but the acme of discomfort is to lie upon a convexity. Persons who have omitted to make a shapely lair for themselves, should at least scrape a hollow in the ground, just where the hip-bone would otherwise press.

The annexed sketch (fig. 1) represents a man sleeping in a natural attitude. It will be observed that he fits into a concavity of about 6 inches in greatest depth. (The scale on which he is drawn is 6 feet long and 1 foot high.)

Galton

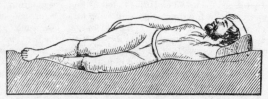

Fig. 1.

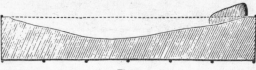

Fig. 2.

Wet Clothes, to dry. — *Fire for drying Clothes.* — To dry clothes it is a very convenient plan to make a dome-shaped frame-work of twigs over a smouldering fire; by bending each twig or wand into a half-circle, and planting both ends of it in the ground, one on each side of the fire. The wet clothes are laid on this framework, and receive the full benefit of the heat. Their steam passes readily upwards.

To keep Clothes from the wet. — Mr. Parkyns says, "I may as well tell, also, how we managed to keep our clothes dry when travelling in the rain: this was rather an important consideration, seeing that each man's wardrobe consisted of what he carried on his back. Our method was at once effective and simple: if halting, we took off our clothes and sat on them; if riding, they were placed under the leathern shabraque of the mule's saddle, or under any article of similar material, bed or bag, that lay on the camel's pack. A good shower-bath did none of us any harm; and as soon as the rain was over, and the moisture on our skins had evaporated, we had our garments as warm, dry, and comfortable, as if they had been before a fire. In populous districts, we kept on our drawers, or supplied their place with a piece of rag, or a skin; and then, when the rain was over, we wrapped ourselves up in our 'quarry,' and taking off the wetted articles, hung them over the animal's cruppers to dry." Another traveller writes:—

"The only means we had of preserving our sole suit of clothes dry from the drenching showers of rain, was by taking them off and stuffing them into the hollow of a tree, which, in the darkness of the night, we could do with propriety."

Galton

Washing Clothes.— *Substitute for Soap.*— The lye of ashes and the gall of animals are the readiest substitutes for soap. The sailor's recipe for washing clothes is well known, but it is too dirty to describe.

Galton

Soap-boiling is not so easy as may be imagined. It requires not only much attention, but the quality is dependent upon the proper mixture of the alkalies. Sixty parts of potash and forty of lime are, I believe, the proportions for common soap. I had neither lime nor potash, but I shortly procured both. The *Hegleck tree (Balanites egyptiaca)* was extremely rich in potash; therefore I burned a large quantity, and made a strong ley with the ashes. This I concentrated by boiling. There was no limestone; but the river produced a plentiful supply of large oyster-shells, that, if burned, would yield excellent lime; accordingly, I constructed a kiln with the assistance of the white ants. The country was infested by these creatures, which erected their dwellings in all directions. There were cones from six to ten feet high, formed of clay, so thoroughly cemented by a glutinous preparation of the insects that it was harder than sun-baked brick. I selected an egg-shaped hill, and cut off the top exactly as we take off the slice from an egg. My Tookrooris then worked hard, and with a hoe and their lances they hollowed it out to the base, in spite of the attacks of the ants, which punished the legs of the intruders considerably. I made a draught hole from the outside base at right angles with the bottom of the hollow cone. My kiln was perfect. I loaded it with wood, upon which I piled about six bushels of oyster-shells, which I then covered with fuel, and kept it burning for twenty-four hours. This produced excellent lime, and I commenced my soap-boiling. We possessed an immense copper pot, of Egyptian manufacture, in addition to a large and deep copper basin, called a *"teshti"*. These would contain about ten gallons. The ley having been boiled down to great strength, I added a quantity of lime and the necessary fat. It required ten hours' boiling, combined with careful management of the fire, as it would frequently ascend like foam, and overflow the edge of the utensils; however, at length having been constantly stirred, it turned to soap; before it became cold I formed it into cakes and balls with my hands, and the result of this manufacture was a weight of about forty pounds of most excellent soap, of a very sporting description, *"Savon à la bête feroce."* We thus washed with rhinoceros soap; our lamp was trimmed with oil of lions; our butter for cooking purposes was the fat of hippopotami, while our pomade was made from the marrow of buffaloes and antelopes, scented with the blossoms of mimosas. We were entirely independent, as our whole party had subsisted upon the produce of the rod and the rifle.

Baker:
Abyssinia

INVALID BATH. If a long bath is not at hand, put a blanket over a waterproof sheet, and let the patient lie on it; get six or eight boys to hold up the edges, and give patient his bath in that way.

William Henry Crosse, M.D., c. 1890.

A traveller when the last of his watches breaks down, has no need to be disheartened from going on with his longitude observations, especially if he observes occultations and eclipses. The object of a watch is to tell the number of seconds that elapse between the instant of occultation, eclipse, &c., and that, a minute or two later, when the sextant observation for time is made; and all that it actually *does*, is to beat seconds and to record the number of beats. Now a string and a stone swung as a pendulum will beat time; and a native who is taught to throw a pebble into a bag at each beat will record it; and for operations that are not tedious, he will be as good as a watch.

Galton

A Hippopotamus Trap

The hippopotami live in families or small herds of from half a dozen to twenty each, basking upon the sandbanks in the tropic sun, bathing in the depths and raising their clumsy-looking equine heads above the surface to look out, or taking nightly walks for miles into the country to crop the herbage of some favourite spot. Taking advantage of the prowling habits of the animal, the natives construct in his path or run, a harpoon trap or drop. The illustration will serve to show the manner in which this contrivance is arranged. The instant the ground cord is detached from its hold by the advancing foot of the hippopotamus, the heavy beam holding the barbed iron drops with tremendous force, and fixes the spear-head deeply in the flesh beneath the tough skin of the victim, who rarely escapes with his life.

Lord & Baines

When an African bull elephant advances in full charge with his ears cocked, his head measures about fourteen feet from the tip of one ear to that of the other, in a direct line across the forehead. I have frequently cut off the ear to form a mat, upon which I have slept beneath the shade of a tree, while my people divided the animal.

Baker:
Abyssinia

Survival Techniques

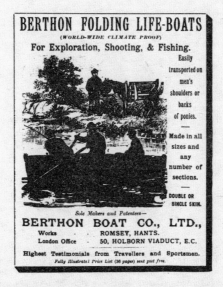

It is a pity that none of the waterproof materials at present in use are comfortable in ordinary wear, so that some common article of dress, as a necktie, a belt, or sash, might be made so as to be inflatable when an accident occurs.

Since writing the above we have been shewn an inflatable silk cravat, which can be worn in the usual way when not required as a float; when charged with air through a small mouthpiece and stop it takes the form of a large sausage, which, surrounding the neck and resting under the chin, serves to keep the head above water, and renders sinking next to impossible. These contrivances are to be obtained at the "Explorer's Room", Cornhill.

Lord & Baines

For Personal Defence

Double Barrelled Pocket Pistols, with Detonating Locks and Spring Bayonets, are best, particularly those which have both barrels above, and do not require turning.

Pocket Door Bolts, which are applicable to almost all sorts of Doors, may on many occasions save the Property and the Life of the Traveller: it is advisable to be always provided with such Bolts:— *The Cork-screw Door-fastening* is the simplest that we have seen; this is screwed in between the Door and the Door-Post, and unites them so firmly, that great power is required to force a Door so fastened. They are as portable as common Corkscrews, and their Weight does not exceed an Ounce and a half.

The safety of your Bed Room Door should always be carefully examined; and in case of Bolts not being at hand, it will be useful to hinder entrance into the Room, by putting a Table and Chair upon it against the Door; such precautions are, however, less necessary in England than they are on the Continent, where it is advisable to choose a Room with Two Beds, and to let your Servant sleep in the Room, and to burn a light all Night:— when you enter the room to go to rest, take a peep behind and under the Beds, Closets, &c. and all places where concealment is possible.

Kitchiner

Fill the Water-vessels.— Never mind what the natives may tell you concerning the existence of water on the road, believe nothing, but resolutely determine to fill the girbas (water-vessels).

Baker:
Abyssinia

On being informed that we had arrived at our halting-place, I made the inquiry most natural to a thirsty man — Where is the water? To which our guide replied by scraping a hole with his hands in the sand, which soon became half full of a dingy, suspicious-looking aqueous matter, which, however, he assured me would (like many young men in Europe) become more respectable when settled.

Parkyns:
Abyssinia

In cases of extreme necessity, and when the preservation of human life depends on the obtainment of water, the supply to be found in the stomach of the camel should not be overlooked or forgotten.

During the Algerian campaign the French made some investigations in order to find out the quantity of water a dead camel's stomach would contain, and the result was that about 15 pints was the average arrived at. This water, although green and turbid, had no offensive smell. It is asserted by the Arabs that water of this character requires three days to clear itself. People, however, dying of thirst, are not very nice.

In all cases of extreme scarcity of food, we strongly advise the traveller to leave no stone unturned which may yield aliment of some kind to help him on his way before he sacrifices his riding horse or mule. Where a number of animals accompany an expedition, a few may perhaps be parted with from time to time; but we earnestly advise the solitary hunter or explorer to exercise every faculty he possesses for food finding before he makes up his mind to destroy his four-footed friend.

Lord & Baines

On another occasion, while exploring a branch of the Victoria River, in North Australia, we halted, as usual, at noon, with scanty rations, which Mr. Gregory improved by taking from his hat a stout sewing needle, softening it in the fire, and bending it into a fish-hook, baited with grasshoppers; a few strands of thread made a sufficiently strong line, a small sapling formed a rod, and, in a few minutes, he had caught three fish, resembling mullet, nearly 18in. long. The needle had done good service, but was too precious to be thrown away, so Mr. Gregory carefully restored it to its pristine straightness, tempered it, and again stuck it in his hat, to be used, when required, for its legitimate purpose.

Lord & Baines

Keeping Warm
In Ashes of Camp Fire. — A few chill hours may be got over, in a plain that affords no other shelter, by nestling among the ashes of a recently burnt-out camp fire.

Warm Carcases. — In Napoleon's retreat, after his campaign in Russia, many a soldier saved or prolonged his life by creeping within the warm and reeking carcase of a horse that had died by the way.

For Alpine ropes, only three sorts of knots are ever required, and we suggest one of each kind:— No. 1 is for the purpose of joining two ends. No. 2 is for the purpose of making a loop at one end. No. 3 is for the purpose of making a loop in the middle when the ends are fastened. No. 4 is a knot, of which we give a diagram *in order that no one may imitate it.*

Galton

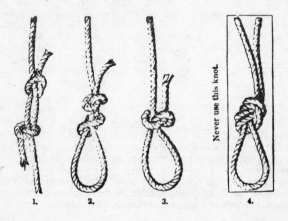

1.   2.   3.   4.

A *ruse* should be borne in mind, that has been practised in most countries, from England to Peru. A traveller is threatened by a robber with a gun, and ordered to throw himself on the ground, or he will be fired at. The traveller taking a pistol from his belt, shouts out, "If this were loaded you should not treat me thus!" and throws himself on the ground as the robber bids him. There he lies till the robber, in his triumph, comes up for his booty; when the intended victim takes a quick aim and shoots him dead — the pistol being really loaded all the time.

Galton

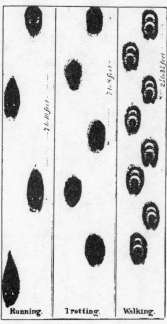

Running.   Trotting.   Walking.

HORSE-TRACKS AT ORDINARY SPEED.

Useful Phrases

In a Fire.

Fire! Fire!

The house is on fire.

Go and fetch the fire engine.

Fill the buckets with water.

Make the ring.

Cut down this wall or this partition with a hatchet.

Let us all set to work.

Take away this little box.

Save all my papers.

There is the key.

Bring a ladder.

Get away. Make haste.

The fire is in the chimney.

Put a wet cloth before the chimney.

The chimney has not been swept for these six months past.

You should get the chimneys swept every two months.

It is difficult to find chimney-sweepers here.

Then fasten a thorn-fagot to the top of a pole, introduce it in the chimney, and by that means, you can sweep it yourself.

Is the fire out.

Do not be afraid, madam, the fire has caught your gown.

Do not move, stay where you are, lay down upon the floor, you will stop the fire with your hands.

Lay upon that canopy, upon that bed, stop the fire with that pillow.

The fire is stopt.

My hands are burnt.

Put honey or grated potatoes upon them.

Madame de Genlis:
'Manuel de Voyageur; or, The Traveller's Pocket Companion', 1816

Propriety

As to the work of undressing and dressing, however, this is managed in a very decent manner. If there were men so brutal as not to go upon deck, and leave the women to themselves, the Captain would instantly interfere, and compel them to do it. However, this is what never happens, I believe. The greatest and most injurious inconvenience is, that the modesty of English women too frequently restrains them from relieving themselves by going to the usual place for the purpose, which place is, and must be, upon the deck, and within the sight of all those who are upon the deck. This reluctance, however amiable in itself (and very amiable it is), has often produced very disagreeable, not to say fatal consequences. That mode of relief has been pointed out by nature; it is indispensable to animal existence; retention to a certain extent is destructive; and the sufferings experienced on this account are very great. *French* women must be excellent sailors; but English women, or American women, must change their natures, before this can cease to be a subject of really serious importance. Use every argument in your power to get over this difficulty with regard to your wife; lose no opportunity of overcoming her scruples; be very attentive to her in every circumstance and point attending this matter; and, if she be in a state, from her sea-sickness, (which is frequently the case) not to admit of removal from her bed, you must be prepared, not only with the utensil suitable to the case, but you yourself must perform the office of chamber-maid; and this, you will observe, must be the case in many instances, whether you be in the steerage or the cabin; for, as to her servant maid, if she have one, you are pretty lucky if you have not to perform the same office for her; for there is no woman on board able to go to her: a thousand to one they are all sick together; and as to any other man performing the office for her, where is such a man to be found?

Cobbett

117

Note.— The modesty of the Indians is very great. Their noble chief, De Campsie, being at a party once where English ladies were showing off their snowy necks and lovely heaving bosoms, on being asked what he thought of them, replied, shaking his head, "They show much too great face for me."

John Mactaggart:
'Three Years in Canada', 1829

Ladies may visit the better-class cafes without dread at least during the day.

Baedecker:
Southern France, 1907

PARTIES GOING ASHORE.— No lady should ever attempt to land at any port of call without the protection of a male escort. When a lady may be unmarried, or travelling without her husband, she should arrange to form one of a party that may be going ashore. Some little tact and experience is required in making up a party that should, if possible, comprise people of congenial tastes; and pre-arrangement of plans is also advisable, as it is awkward on landing to find one lady "bent" on shopping while another wants to go sight-seeing. The party should never be too large, should always include one or more gentlemen, and young ladies should be properly chaperoned. "Mrs. Grundy" is duly represented in all tropical countries, and, on board ship especially, a woman cannot be too careful of what she says or does, as her smallest words and actions are liable to be made the subject of comment and tittle-tattle.

Major S. Leigh Hunt & Alexander S. Kenny:
'Tropical Trials — A Hand-Book for Women in the Tropics', 1883

As soon as the anchor was dropped, a number of apparently naked savages doubtless swarmed on board the steamer, from the boats alongside, and but that he knew beforehand how peaceful were their intentions, and saw they were unarmed, the apparition might have given rise to horrible visions of cannibalism, or at the very least of scalping. The attire of these specimens of humanity is somewhat scanty, certainly, but as far as coolness goes, admirably suited to the climate. It may be described as consisting of a coloured handkerchief tied round the head, and a small piece of cotton cloth, or perhaps another handkerchief, round the loins.

Such is the garb in which some dozen muscular, well-formed, mustachioed men suddenly present themselves before the passengers of every newly arrived vessel, and the result is no doubt to produce in some cases a slight shock to the susceptibilities. But we soon get accustomed to this sort of thing in India: indeed so much accustomed, that ultimately most people fail to see anything at all capable of reform or improvement in this neglect of clothing, which at least is hardly refined.

Probably the dark skin goes a great way towards weakening the effect, for the same degree of nudity in a white man would undoubtedly be far from reconcilable with average European ideas of propriety. But "use is second nature," and what causes native nakedness soon to cease attracting any attention, is its universality among the lower orders, manifestly without the least thought of impropriety.

Hull:
India

Both sexes bathe almost in the same place, the men lying on their backs in about nine inches of water, and the women sitting in a hole about ten yards below them. Most of the women and all the men were quite naked; so it may be imagined that this style of bathing would not altogether suit the ideas of the frequenters of Bath or Cheltenham, though in these latitudes such little naturalities are not objected to.

Parkyns:
Abyssinia

It will hardly be credited that, while this Alameda is crowded with people, women of all ages, without clothes of any sort or kind, are bathing in great numbers in the stream which literally bounds the promenade. Shakespeare tells us, that "the chariest maid is prodigal enough if she unveil her beauties to the moon," but the ladies of Mendoza, not contented with this, appear even before the sun; and in the mornings and evenings they really bathe without any clothes in the Rio de Mendoza, the water of which is seldom up to their knees, the men and women all together; and certainly, of all the scenes which in my life I have witnessed, I never beheld one so indescribable.

Captain F. B. Head:
'Rough Notes taken during some rapid Journeys across the Pampas and among the Andes', 1828

Recreations

THE "SPORTS" (from a sketch by G. A. Musgrave)

On Board Ship

Our second-class fellow-passengers commenced the concert season by giving a very amusing entertainment in their saloon. The first piece on the programme was an "overture by the band" — the band being represented by a single concertina. The chairman, a jolly-looking old tar, tried three pieces, and broke down in all, amidst roars of laughter and calls for the chorus. An "ancient buffer" sang "My Pretty Jane," and a few other sentimental things, with looks of fond affection. Then came a solo by "Bones," and another sailor gave a song which recounted his many ailments. He said he had had "brownchitis," "scarlatina," "concertina," and "tightness in the chest." Then a melancholy youth ground out something about his love for a "Little brown jug," calling frequently for a chorus, the whole ending with "God save the Queen."

Tangye

Society

Much hospitality is shown to tourists in India, and they should therefore be prepared, particularly if they have letters of introduction, for dinner-parties and dances.

The Imperial Guide to India 1904.

Useful Phrases

Supper.

Gentlemen, supper is ready.

Let us make haste, as it is late. We must get up very early to-morow morning.

I have no appetite; I could willingly go to bed without any supper.

Your appetite will improve as you eat. Come, come, there is some agreeable society, you will be amused.

Good evening, Gentlemen. Oh! Lord A., are you here! What has brought you into this country?

I have just come from Italy with my wife and the Marquis.

Lady A., I have the honour to present my respects to you. How did you enjoy yourself in Italy? Did you like the country?

Yes, extremely. We were there three months without being dull for a single moment. I could have stayed there a year.

Let us sit down; the supper is getting cold. We can talk at supper.

Sit here beside my wife. And you, Sir, here between the lady and me.

I shall be very well placed here opposite the Countess.

Will you allow me to help you to some vermicelli.

No, thank you. I ate it so good in Italy, that I do not choose to run the risk of eating it bad in France.

Yes, that is true, vermicelli (farinaceous food) is excellent in Italy.

I will thank you for a little of that fried fish.

It is excellent.

Baedecker's Traveller's Manual of Conversation in Four Languages, 1886

Cadiz, though fast declining from the wealth and splendour to which she had reached during her exclusive privilege to trade with the colonies, is still one of the few towns in Spain, which, for refinement, can be compared with some of the second-rate in England. The people are hospitable and cheerful. The women, without being at all beautiful, are really fascinating. Some of the *tertulias,* or evening parties, which a simple introduction to the lady of the house entitles any one to attend daily, are very lively and agreeable. No stiffness of etiquette prevails: you may drop in when you like, and leave the room when it suits you. Singing to the guitar or the piano, is a very common resource at these meetings; but the musical acquirements of the Spanish ladies cannot bear the most distant comparison with those of the female amateurs in London.

Rev. J. Blanco White:
'Letters from Spain by Don Leucacio Doblado', 1822

Displays

The howling Dervishes have been banished to Scutary, where they exhibit in secret every Thursday, their disgusting mummery, for which a small sum must be paid by a stranger, to enable him to witness it.

Levinge

COMBAT DES ANIMAUX, Barrière du Combat.— This exhibition, which is only held on Sundays, Mondays, and festivals, is consecrated to the genius of vulgarity and ferocity, whose disciples preside at the ceremonies, in the shape of butchers, carmen, etc. The exhibition consists of an enclosure, round which there is a gallery, and under it dens of beasts, together with a kennel of dogs, who are always ready for battle. Wolves, bulls, and bears, the latter with their teeth filed down, encounter trained dogs; but the latter seldom kill their opponents, as amusement, not destruction, instigates the combats. The bulls have their horns sawn off. There are also fire-works exhibited, in which is to be seen a bull-dog raised 50 feet by a rope, which he holds between his teeth, regardless of the flames which surround him. The spectacle commences at 3 to 4 o'clock. Admittance 1fr. and 2 fr.

Galignani's Guide of Paris, 1841

Repugnant as slavery is to the feelings of an Englishman, few travellers pass through Cairo without visiting the slave bazaar, where men, women and children are to be seen exposed for sale like so many brute creatures: happily however these markets do not exhibit the melancholy spectacle that imagination would lead one to expect in such a scene of wretchedness.

Hints to Overland Travellers (From India — via Egypt) 1838.

Constantinople: The (slave) market is open every day, but on Saturdays the greater number of slaves is exposed. Any one may enter but no Christian is permitted to become the purchaser of a slave. A Mohammedan friend must buy for him, which is frequently done.

Levinge

Having a great desire to see the far-famed guillotine, I had taken considerable pains to be forewarned of the first occasion, when it was expected "to perform." Great efforts are used to hinder the publicity of an execution, while, at the same time, those who desire to witness it are not prevented. The criminal, when sentenced to death, is left in ignorance of the day of his dreadful doom. The public are also uninformed. His sentence is made known in the gazettes of the day, but he generally suffers three days afterwards. It is said, that neither the jailor nor hangman know the precise time, till the previous night, when they suddenly receive orders to erect the scaffold. The prisoner is sometimes reprieved, and this for one month only. I had engaged a workman who labours near the barrier St. Jaques — an unfrequented part of the city — to send me word when he observed preparations going on in the square. The guillotine is always erected between eleven and twelve o'clock on the night previous to the execution.

I was therefore aroused by his messenger at six o'clock a.m. I made such good haste, that I was dressed and on the spot at twenty minutes past six — having arrived there by running all the way, about two miles. I found quite a crowd already assembled, but it being some time before the fatal hour, I had leisure to inspect the instrument minutely. On a platform erected four or five feet above the ground, supported by legs and surrounded by a railing, was a frame-work rising to the height of between eight or ten feet. Those who have witnessed the operation of a spile-driver, will conceive a very good idea of its action and appearance. The whole was painted red. The cutting instrument resembled a Yankee hay-cutter, except that it was much larger. One corner, being placed lower down than the other, facilitated its operation. The axe, or knife, was fixed into a heavy block of metal, and drawn up nearly to the top of the frame. There it remained dull and sullen, like revenge awaiting its opportunity. Two companies of mounted municipal guards, and one of foot, with some twenty *Sergents de ville*, kept the square open till eight o'clock, the fixed hour. In the meantime the crowd augmented, and the women began to be quite numerous. One old woman was peddling a biography of the victim, and another endeavouring to let her stands and chairs, both screaming their merchandize at the top of their voices.

At eight o'clock precisely came the guard of cavalry at a fast trot, surrounding the covered cart, which contained the prisoner and a priest. The vehicle was backed up to the scaffold, the door behind was opened, the priest descended, and after him the criminal. The latter mounted the scaffold, accompanied by two officers, with a firm step. He was clothed in his usual dress, a blouse of blue cloth, but without a hat. The hair was cut short, that it might form no impediment to his speedy exit from the world. The officers quickly drew the blouse over his head, and he stood exposed with naked shoulders. He then began to scream with the intention of making himself heard by the crowd, as I thought, but like many unaccustomed orators, ignorant how to use his voice. It might have been an ebullition of either anger or fear. In France the liberty of speech is not permitted, and he was interrupted by the officers bending his neck, and placing his head in the groove destined to receive it. The collar, which was intended to check the least movement, was adjusted, and like the weight in the spile-driver on our wharves, the axe was drawn up to the top by the officers. It was instantly disengaged, and dropped: the head, dis-severed completely, fell into a basket; and this officer's duty being finished, he descended. Two minutes did not elapse from the time he arrived, till his head was detached from his body. Without the smallest loss of time it was tumbled into a vehicle, similar to a hay-cart, his body tipped in after, a small guard escorted it beyond the barrier, and in five minutes from the entrance of the prisoner he was borne away, and the place left nearly vacant. — The body was conveyed away for interment without the city for some hour or two, to be dug up again, and carried to the dissecting-room for anatomical purposes.

There are many methods of leaving the world, but I cannot imagine one which could be less painful and more agreeable than this — if any method of dying may be styled so; — with the single, but rather unpleasant exception of the scaffold, none certainly could be more expeditious. How much superior to hanging, where the criminal struggles long and hard often from the ignorance of carelessness of the hangman! From the guillotine, no pain can possibly be experienced.

Amateurs can see the operation of this celebrated instrument on a dog for twenty francs, on giving notice of their desire to the officer a week in advance. Jack Ketches* of other countries have free admittance.

*[Executioners]

Augustus Kinsley Gardner, M.D.:
'Old Wine in New Bottles', 1849

Pig-sticking.— No sport in the world can provide quite the same sensation as riding on the tail of a pig. Nothing can be more enjoyable than your first drink as you stand panting with exertion and pouring with sweat over a fine tusker. It differs from English fox-hunting in that you do not choose your own line. The pig does that, and you "see red" and ride like the devil. You must keep your eye glued on that pig's tail and not on the country, and all you can do is to pull your horse together a bit for an obstacle. Those with you will, unless their pig-craft may suggest some better plan, ride parallel in case he "jinks".

You raise your spear high up, so that he who runs may read that you are the man on the tail of the pig and can see him still. In some stations pig-sticking is spoiled by the man who "rides for the spear". It is *not* good form to ride your pal off to spear as you do at polo. You are out in combination against the pig, and if you don't combine in heavy country you'll lose a lot. Get a good horse if you can, but if you can't, get a handy one, and you'll have good sport in any but big stations like Meerut. Use your head and your eyes. Nothing requires greater concentration to my mind than calculating your chances on the pig's action in difficult country. You won't learn the art in a day, or a month, or a season, but when you have, you'll like nothing better.

Lieut. J. E. Power 19th Lancers (F.H.) Indian Army:
'Vade Mecum for Officers and Civilians Proceeding to India', 1912

The English Abroad

At Ismaïlia we stopped some time, and a lad wanted to clean my boots which, however, did not require cleaning, so I told him to black the bare feet of a brown boy who was standing by. This he proceeded to do in the presence of a crowd of grinning spectators of all colours — yellow, brown, coffee-coloured, and jet black. The lad whose feet were blacked seemed to enjoy the fun very much, and when it was over appeared to think he was entitled to a half piastre as well as the operator, so he got it. The shoeblack then brought an ebony Nubian, whose skin was already a shining black. He asked me if he might do his feet, but I made him understand it was quite unnecessary. A grave-looking Turk observing the proceedings gave a look which seemed to say, "Mad English again."

Tangye

125

The Traveller's Duty

Many travellers adopt the practice of taking a soldier from the chief or king of the country in which they may be travelling, to ensure them a hospitable reception in the villages where they may be obliged to lodge. Many also, thus provided, affect a harsh demeanour to the natives, demanding lodging, food, &c., in the most peremptory manner. Now this, in my opinion, is a plan not at all to be recommended. In the first place, it often leads to a quarrel, which is a disagreeable introduction into a village, and not a likely one to obtain for a traveller what he ought so much to court if he wishes to study the manners and customs of a people — their good will and confidence. Secondly, to have an Amhàra soldier with you, or in fact to be supposed to have anything to do with the camp or people of Oubi, is no recommendation to the confidence of the Tigrèans; nor is it at all a likely means to induce them to open their hearts, or let their feelings, especially on political subjects, be known to you, by thus appearing before them under the protection of and accompanied by a soldier from the household of their tyrannical usurper. Thirdly, "Every man's house is his castle." I should very much dislike any one's forcing himself into my house, against my will, and am disposed to act generally on the principle of "Do unto others as ye would they should do unto you." Travellers should learn, like Rasselas and Nekayah, "to understand that they have for a time laid aside their dignity, and are to expect only such regard as liberality and courtesy can procure." There's nothing like a civil tongue and quiet unpretending manners to get one on in these countries, as I suppose in all others. On my arrival at a village I have always found it the better plan to do as native travellers would — wait under a tree till some one asks me in. This is generally soon done, though a little patience is sometimes needed. People often gather round you to look at you, and occasionally make rather personal remarks, though generally they are very civil. Only answer their questions good-naturedly, and take pleasure in making yourself agreeable, which you will find will become a habit, and you will be welcome everywhere. I don't think it necessary to mention, as some travellers do, every place I slept in, and what I was fed with every day, but sometimes I must be allowed to do so, hoping that a few instances of the way in which I was treated, without any bullying on my part, may induce some future traveller to think like myself, that it is not absolutely necessary to enter forcibly into other people's houses, or to demand as a right the supper which one ought to receive with thanks if voluntarily given. What right has Oubi to make his peasantry feed me or any one else? They pay their taxes, whether or no: and if he were generously disposed towards strangers, why does he not supply them at his own expense? I have said a good deal on this subject, because I have not only heard people express their opinion that force, or rather authority, was necessary for a man to make his way in some countries, but I have even seen similar opinions published.

Parkyns:
Abyssinia

These notes on Odessa cannot be closed without some allusion to certain of its sights and scenes, with which strangers in general are but too familiar, and which would merit to be spoken of in a very different tone from that hitherto employed in this chapter. In fact, every town in Russia contains scenes of the most disgusting profligacy; and they are now referred to for the double purpose of satisfying those who, knowing Russia, would be surprised to find no notice taken of them in these pages, and at the same time of warning our travelling countrymen that both in Russia, and in other parts of the continent, they ought to shun those haunts, if not out of respect for themselves, at least out of respect for their country, the character of which has too often suffered by the conduct of those who leave our shores. Even individuals who at home would shudder at the idea of coming in contact with vice, often throw aside their scruples when abroad, on the plea that it is a traveller's duty to see everything. The plea, however, is inadmissible: it is the traveller's duty to see all that is distinctive, peculiar, or new, in the countries he visits; but, as we have never heard that vice and immorality are very rare in any part of the world, he cannot with reason plead the attraction of novelty, as an excuse for wilfully seeking such sights. The traveller's object ought to be to find out what is good in foreign countries, rather than what is bad. Instead of the foul and degrading recollections of the nature now alluded to, he ought to try to carry away some happy and improving remembrance, to bind him in after-days with each land he has visited.

Bremner:
Russia

It ought to be part of our patriotic feeling to endeavour to convey as agreeablé an idea as possible of ourselves to those countries which we honour with our distinguished presence in our little trips.

Mrs. C. E. Humphries:
'Manners For Women', 1897